T0152228

Growing Together in Christ

DISCLAIMER

No part of this publication may be reproduced or transmitted in any form or by any means, mechanical or electronic, including photocopying or recording, or by any information storage and retrieval system, or transmitted by email without permission in writing from the author. Neither the author nor the publisher assumes any responsibility for errors, omissions, or contrary interpretations of the subject matter herein. Any perceived slight of any individual or organization is purely unintentional. Brand and product names are trademarks or registered trademarks of their respective owners.

GROWING TOGETHER IN CHRIST

The Maximized Couple's Guide
to a Stronger Devotional Life

WILLIAM HUTCHESON

NASHVILLE

NEW YORK • LONDON • MELBOURNE • VANCOUVER

GROWING TOGETHER IN CHRIST
The Maximized Couple's Guide to a Stronger Devotional Life

© 2021 William Hutcheson

All rights reserved. No portion of this book may be reproduced, stored in a retrieval system, or transmitted in any form or by any means—electronic, mechanical, photocopy, recording, scanning, or other—except for brief quotations in critical reviews or articles, without the prior written permission of the publisher.

Published in New York, New York, by Morgan James Publishing. Morgan James is a trademark of Morgan James, LLC. www.MorganJamesPublishing.com

Morgan James BOGO™

A **FREE** ebook edition is available for you or a friend with the purchase of this print book.

CLEARLY SIGN YOUR NAME ABOVE

Instructions to claim your free ebook edition:
1. Visit MorganJamesBOGO.com
2. Sign your name CLEARLY in the space above
3. Complete the form and submit a photo of this entire page
4. You or your friend can download the ebook to your preferred device

ISBN 9781631953736 paperback
ISBN 9781631953743 eBook
Library of Congress Control Number:
2020948535

Cover Design by:
Rachel Lopez
www.r2cdesign.com

Interior Design by:
Christopher Kirk
www.GFSstudio.com

Scripture marked KJV is taken from the King James Version of the Holy Bible. Scripture marked NIV is taken from the Holy Bible, New International Version®, NIV® Copyright ©1973, 1978, 1984, 2011 by Biblica, Inc.® Used by permission. All rights reserved worldwide. Scripture marked NLT is taken from the *Holy Bible*, New Living Translation, copyright © 1996, 2004, 2015 by Tyndale House Foundation. Used by permission of Tyndale House Publishers, Inc., Carol Stream, Illinois 60188. All rights reserved. Scripture marked The Voice is taken from The Voice Bible Copyright © 2012 Thomas Nelson, Inc. The Voice™ translation © 2012 Ecclesia Bible Society. All rights reserved.

Morgan James is a proud partner of Habitat for Humanity Peninsula and Greater Williamsburg. Partners in building since 2006.

Get involved today! Visit
MorganJamesPublishing.com/giving-back

CONTENTS

CHAPTER 1:

The Undercurrent

Jessica expected to feel great contentment; instead she felt an undercurrent swirling in her soul. This quiet Sunday afternoon offered a rare moment of unhurried reflection. She ran down a mental checklist: "The job goes well. I've hit loan app targets the last several months, and my boss is pleased." She continued with, "I'm healthy, according to my latest physical." Next she moved to the family. "I am blessed! My family is well. The children are in a good place right now, doing well in school and still going to church, and I'm so pleased with our marriage. Rich and I have always had a good relationship, but we thought our relationship could improve. Now our relationship is the best it has been in years, after our marriage coaching."

Jess ruminated on the marriage coaching experience she and Rich recently finished. She began coaching with more anxiety and uncertainty than she admitted to either Rich or Bill, their coach. Just as Bill assured them, marriage coaching proved to be a straightforward process, determining where their marriage stood and where they thought God wanted them to go. It was a process that helped Jess and Rich move toward their goal. Bill asked questions that led to surprising answers, and he sometimes offered Jess and Rich a thought or challenge they hadn't expected, but there were no surprise punches.

Yes, coaching required transparency and effort, but Jess realized they made more significant gains in their marriage in that short season than in any period of their relationship. Jess entered coaching with the belief that an up-leveled marriage would satisfy her soul. She thought that would bring a sense of peace, so where was that peace?

"Why do I feel unsettled?" Jess wondered. "Why has this vague dissatisfaction reappeared? Deep down, in my soul, I feel an undercurrent that will not give me peace. What's wrong?"

Jess could admit this to herself, but how could she tell Rich? He started coaching because Jess asked. After the first couple of sessions, Rich confessed that coaching may be helpful. By the end of the last session, Rich thanked Bill for the great strides he and Jess had made. Rich was elated, so how could Jess say to Rich, "I want more"?

Jess's mind played the scene like this: she'd say she still felt that they needed more, and Rich would react negatively. She imagined he would also take it personally as if she were dissatisfied with him.

That was the last thing Jess wanted to communicate. She felt profound gratitude to God for putting her and Rich together, and she couldn't be more satisfied with him as a husband, friend, and companion.

"No!" Jess thought. "I don't want to hurt him, but I remember how Bill brought up our couple devotional life in the second-to-last session. Something clicked at that moment. We talked about how our individual devotional lives were strong, but how we rarely shared our faith together, as a couple. I knew something important was missing in my—in our—life at that point. The next week the undercurrent of dissatisfaction reappeared."

Jess sought help from God to understand the dissatisfaction and how to approach Rich.

After a few minutes, a thought crystallized in her mind. Their coaching afforded marked improvement in their emotional and physical intimacy. Yet they lacked intimacy in the most crucial marriage area—their spiritual life! The moment that realization appeared, Jess knew why she still felt "unfinished" and how to approach Rich.

Jess prayerfully hatched a plan. She would engage Rich in conversation about their coaching experience. Then she would bring up Bill's discussion about the missing ingredient—a couple's devotional life. She would express how God may be "nudging her," as Bill would say, in that direction.

She would continue by saying that she felt "exposed" or unprepared for difficult future events. She wondered how she and Rich would fare if something painful or tragic occurred. Would their individual devotional lives be enough? Wouldn't they be much better off to learn how to walk together spiritually now? Jess felt a bit bolder after rehearsing the conversation in her mind.

After prayer, Jess approached Rich. He had been reading the paper in his recliner, and Jess sat across from him in her recliner. After a moment, Jess began. "Rich, honey, I've been thinking." Rich lowered the paper, waiting for her next comments. "Do you remember, in the second-to-last coaching session with Bill, when he mentioned one missing ingredient in our marriage—a devotional life as a couple?"

Rich put down the paper. He paused, making Jess a bit nervous as she thought he might squelch the conversation at the start. Instead he replied, "Have you been thinking about that too?"

Jess smiled and exhaled a big "Yes!"

Jess and Rich shared their thoughts and found that their minds traveled in parallel directions. Both sensed that missing dimension in their marriage but didn't know how to discuss it. Rich admitted feeling a bit of guilt for his lack of a devotional life compared to Jess's. Jess longed for a deeper spiritual intimacy with Rich but didn't want to push. Rich questioned his ability to keep up with Jess, who attended regular Bible studies. He realized that Jess sounded more confident than he when she prayed. Rich's family had no spiritual life outside of attending church a few times each year and for funerals and weddings. Jess grew up in a family that openly shared their faith and regularly attended worship. Rich realized the difference and remarked how spiritually inadequate he felt to share devotions with Jess. But he now wanted them to share their faith life together.

The conversation Jess had dreaded turned out to be encouraging and hopeful. Their first tentative words on the subject opened a healthy dialogue that revealed God's hand leading them to grow together in their devotional life.

What about you? Do you feel that unnamed undercurrent in your soul? Do you sense that something is missing? Do you sense that more is possible in your marriage?

Like Jess and Rich, your marriage may seem fine, but a little worm of discontent is niggling at your heart. You feel content with your husband, so that's not the issue. You're not discontent with your job. Your career could be better, but it's good enough, and you may even enjoy many of your colleagues. You find that your children are doing well, and your own devotional life is growing.

However, what about your devotional life as a couple? Do you want a deeper devotional life with your beloved? What does he or she want? Does your spouse feel a measure of spiritual discontent? How do you broach the subject with your partner?

If your partner expresses a similar desire or is willing to follow you into it, where do you start? What resources are available?

I'm glad you asked these questions. You're holding a resource for that purpose, and it may be unlike anything you've ever read before, but that's for another chapter. First, allow me to share a bit about myself so I can help you and your spouse create a couple's devotional life.

CHAPTER 2:

Sharing My Passion as a Fellow Pilgrim

If I've not had the privilege of coaching you, then allow me to introduce myself. My parents gave me the name William Dean Hutcheson, but most people call me Bill. I've been the husband to Mary Beth since January 7, 1978. God blessed us with two wonderful daughters married to two fine men and who have given us three delightful grandchildren. I grew up in the middle of Georgia and was educated there through college. I then traveled to Louisville, Kentucky, for my Master of Divinity (MDiv). While there, I met Mary Beth, the woman who would become my wife. I've served three gracious Baptist congregations in Georgia and retired in 2016, after thirty-six years as pastor.

As my pedigree is now highlighted, you need to know that I am a passionate pilgrim-believer. Let me break that down a bit. First, God gave me a passion for helping believers advance on their spiritual journey toward Him. Outside of loving my family, nothing gives me more satisfaction than witnessing a person progress in his or her spiritual life. No matter what projects I complete, what "successes" I realize along the way, or what accolades come my way, I love seeing God work in someone's life.

Second, I'm on this journey too, and I still have much to learn. My spiritual pilgrimage began at a young age, as my mother took me to church when I was only a few months old. I've been on a church roll and actively involved all my life.

The Holy Spirit wooed me when I was nine. Following my dad's death, I felt the need to "be saved." Our pastor came over to our home and talked me through the meaning and the process of becoming God's child. That afternoon, on our knees in our living room, I surrendered my life.

Of course, I knew nearly nothing about the spiritual life. How could I understand what it meant to grow in grace and practice Spiritual Disciplines? Even so, from that November day in 1963, God gracefully counted me as His son. My understanding of that privilege took time to form. Most of what I've learned about the spiritual life came from a few teachers and divine guidance.

As a pastor, I witnessed the spiritual development of many believers. Also, my pastoral position required that I attend closely to my own spiritual maturity. That meant—and means—growing in dependence on God.

When Mary Beth and I married, I had no idea how God intended our relationship to become the primary tool He would use for our spiritual development. Each of us was still struggling as twenty-somethings to "get a footing" on spiritual soil. We struggled, like most believing couples, to establish our couple's devotional life. Indeed, we spent much of our early marriage years separately having our own devotions.

I began to experience "the undercurrent" about fifteen years into our marriage. My wife, Mary Beth, and I rarely shared devotions together. I mentioned it, and Mary Beth agreed we should have devotional time together. We shared Bible readings and prayer a few times, but they felt awkward, and our effort soon evaporated.

One day, as we ended another strained devotional time, Mary Beth confessed that she felt intimidated. You could have pushed me over with a straw! When I inquired further, she said she felt inadequate. I was the pastor; I had a theological education. Yes, she earned a master's degree in vocal performance at the seminary, but she still felt self-conscious. She didn't believe she understood scripture as well as I did.

Additionally, Mary Beth felt embarrassed to pray in front of me. I didn't realize how she felt; I was unaware of my use of theological language. At that point in our marriage, I didn't know my personality type enjoyed wordsmithing. On the other hand, her personality type found the ease and fluidity of language more difficult. (Learning about personality differences and how they may strengthen or weaken a relationship came a bit later in our marriage. We benefitted from this knowledge so much that I incorporated personality identification as a regular part of my coaching.)

I slowly changed. Eventually, I grew up some and humbled myself, using non-theological language, and I prayed in simpler words. Over time, Mary Beth and I grew to appreciate each other's personalities, gifts, and skills. She developed much more self-confidence. Now our devotional times don't feel awkward. We have prayer daily and often several times a day. We share devotional times much more often and find them significant and satisfying. Our couple's devotional life has improved, but we are still a work in progress.

One of the greatest lessons God granted Mary Beth and me surrounds the realization of spiritual intimacy. I didn't understand the concept of spiritual intimacy until we began to share devotional time together. We knew emotional intimacy; we often shared our feelings, and we enjoyed physical intimacy as God's gift. The word "intimacy" seemed to fit our emotional life and sexual life. Still, it felt odd when attached to the word "spiritual." Then the Spirit helped me realize that intimacy relates to vulnerability and transparency.

Remember the Garden of Eden. The man and woman existed in that idyllic setting, naked and unashamed. Only after they stepped over the only boundary God set did Adam and Eve feel ashamed. What did they do? They sewed together scratchy fig leaves to cover themselves; they hid part of their being. Their action corrupted their intimacy by pushing them toward secrecy and translucence. Humans still feign intimacy, even as they dance the fig-leaf shuffle. The recovery of trust in God and each other and the movement away from secrecy toward transparency leads to intimacy—emotionally, physically, and especially spiritually!

Mary Beth and I changed. We hide less and show more of our incompleteness. We walk the same path as you. Perhaps we've covered a few more miles than you, but we've only done so by God's grace. While we walk the same believers' path, our experiences differ. You may be new to the faith and need some direction to start this couple's devotional life. You and your spouse may share a significantly different spiritual upbringing, and you wish to close the gap between you. As an individual, you may have experienced spiritual renewal and now feel a burning desire to deepen the spiritual life with your beloved. Perhaps you two feel motivated to grow together in the faith because of a change in life circumstances, like a first child, or recovery from a life-threatening illness or accident.

Whatever your reason, I believe God prompted this book. Know that the book you hold represents years of our successes and failures. We share them for one reason: that our transparency and vulnerability may be used by God to encourage your spiritual intimacy.

In that way, we all walk the same path toward the Father. The Spirit helps us know the direction and gives us the strength to walk together as a couple.

Are you ready to journey together? I invite you to travel with me for a spell if you don't mind the company of someone still learning.

CHAPTER 3:

Sailing the Couple's Spiritual Catamaran on the Channels of Grace

Intentionality Is Key

The spiritual life, whether as an individual or couple, flourishes with intention. The idea of discipline depends on intentional actions. You expressed a desire when you purchased this book; you intended to improve your couple's spiritual life. In fact, you took steps to get to this point. Perhaps you Googled "devotionals for couples." You may have searched a bookstore shelf for a book addressing this topic. The step or steps you took brought you to my book. You then purchased it from the bookstore or online, but you didn't stop there. You've now read into the third chapter.

You've taken several concrete steps to fulfill your intention. Spiritual discipline involves the same level of intentionality. Let's translate your vague wish for a couple's devotional life into specific choices and concrete steps in the pages that follow. How? By using Spiritual Disciplines.

Heard of Spiritual Disciplines?

Over the millennia, God revealed the steps through which we can build a life lived in close relationship with Him. We call these steps Spiritual Disciplines. These disciplines may be seen as God's tools to shape us, not our means to manipulate God. You cannot rub the discipline lamp and hope that genie-God will pop out to grant your wishes.

Instead, the disciplines serve as God's means to draw us closer to Himself. Over time, the disciplines may become familiar to us, but we cannot master them. That would be comparable to the tail wagging the dog. No, God uses the disciplines to master us. Do your human sensibilities grouse at that picture? We don't want to be mastered by anyone because of our pride and competitiveness. Yet when we experience the Father's gentle and benevolent mastery, the idea's negative aspects fade. We want to yield to God's rule when we understand the fulfillment of life under Him.

God granted us these disciplines so that, by following them, we can experience the life He intended for us. Therefore, our intentions become a reality by exercising the Spiritual Disciplines! The disciplines below will introduce you to the intentional couple's devotional life.

Steppingstones

The disciplines may be described as steppingstones toward God, or as pipes through which God pours His transforming grace into our lives. Richard Foster writes as one of the premier contemporary thinkers and authors on the Spiritual Disciplines. In his classic, *Celebration of Discipline: The Path to Spiritual Growth*, he states, "The purpose of the Disciplines is liberation from the stifling slavery to self-interest and fear . . . The primary requirement is a longing after God."[1]

Are you ready to be liberated from self-interest and fear? Yes, you arrived here precisely because you desire you and your spouse to become one-in-Spirit, but you didn't know how to begin this process.

Well, that's what I wish to present to you now. The disciplines described below belong to the ages. For millennia, followers of Christ have used them in some form to grow closer to God. Now, as you and your honey

---

1   Richard J. Foster, *Celebration of Discipline: The Path to Spiritual Growth, 20th Anniversary Edition* (San Francisco: HarperSanFrancisco, 1998), 2.

use them, you may expect God to draw you closer to Him and to each other.

Six Disciplines

Through my study of the Spiritual Disciplines, I've identified at least 23 separate steppingstones to God. Richard Foster offers a tidy rubric for organizing the disciplines: the Inward, the Outward, and the Corporate Disciplines. To maintain the parallelism of the triad, I call the last group the Upward Disciplines. Of those, I have chosen six that lay the foundation other disciplines may build upon, two from each of the discipline directions. Every discipline holds an important place, but these disciplines serve as a foundation for the others. Remember, they act as steppingstones on the spiritual path. They show you the way to God, just as steppingstones mark the trail in a garden. You may also use the channel metaphor. These disciplines serve as a means to an end of spiritual growth. Think of them as a funnel, channeling God's grace into and through a believer's life.

I chose the following disciplines: worship, Bible reading, prayer, service, generosity, and gratitude. Each one will be represented in a corresponding chapter, which will present foundational information about each discipline. Much more has been written and spoken about the disciplines. If your curiosity grows concerning one or more of the disciplines included here, or if you wish to know some of the others, I encourage you to search. You will find an abundance of literature on the Spiritual Disciplines. To help you, chapter 13 is a brief list of resources available. Most of them have been instrumental in God's development of my spirit; I commend them to you.

Disciplines and Practice Ahead

Along with explaining each discipline, you will find Devotional Starters to move the discipline from concept to concrete. The combination of information and practice stands as the primary uniqueness of my book. Many books offer detailed information about the disciplines, but they don't provide the reader with suggestions on how to practice them. Other devotional books present inspired material for couples to read and ruminate on together. Still, they usually do not give information that allows you to understand the devotional principles.

At the end of each introduction of a discipline, you will find passages to study together and a simple process to frame your discussions. You will not find background information on each scripture selection. I hope you have a study Bible with book introductions and outlines to fill in those details. This book's scope would not allow for such a study, even though I find it fascinating. You may wish to do that study, or you may simply use the passage as a stand-alone. Know that the preliminary background study on each passage will yield more generous dividends.

Even so, I know most couples just starting this spiritual journey together do so in the middle of hectic schedules. Carving out a short time may require effort and sacrifice. For that reason, I offer a study format that takes as little as ten minutes.

I suspect those who begin these disciplines and who establish a regular shared study time will find ten minutes insufficient. They will likely carve other times out of their schedules to devote to this spiritually beneficial and satisfying study time.

I will give you one caution before we move forward. These disciplines serve as a place to stand with God to receive His grace. In themselves, the disciplines have no power to cause spiritual growth. Going through the motions in a discipline without bringing your full being into the practice will bring no change. Foster had a good thought on this, writing, "the mechanics do not mean that we are practicing the disciplines. The Spiritual Disciplines are an inward and spiritual reality, and the inner attitude of the heart is far more crucial than the mechanics for coming into the reality of the spiritual life."[2] God wants to connect with your hearts. The mechanics provide a structure for expressing your passion to connect with your heavenly Father.

---

2   Richard J. Foster, *Celebration of Discipline: The Path to Spiritual Growth, 20th Anniversary Edition* (San Francisco: HarperSanFrancisco, 1998), 3.

DEVOTIONAL STARTER DIRECTIONS

- Following each of the disciplines, you will find several passages to use as devotional starters. Choose several to practice after you have read the introductory part as a couple.

- I offer this simple four-step structure for your Bible study time. I have used this for years in my devotional time, while Mary Beth and I have used it for a shorter time. I call the following "the four Ps" for obvious reasons. I've seen this same content labeled the S.O.A.P. method, meaning Scripture, Observation, Application, and Prayer. You can "S.O.A.P. up" the four Ps any way that helps you remember. Just do them if you don't have a better method:

  o Passage: Read the passage over a couple of times.

  o Past: What did the author say to the original hearers/readers?

  o Present: What caught my attention in the passage? Share with your spouse.

  o Prayer: Turn the Spirit-impressed thoughts into a prayer.

Let's Start from Scratch

In the next six chapters, I assume you know nothing about these Spiritual Disciplines. More than likely, you already know something about them, but I offer the elemental explanation of each so that we share the same vocabulary and concepts. May these chapters serve to remind you of the disciplines, or may they teach you something, or something more, about them.

Refitting Yourself as a Catamaran

The Christian Spiritual Disciplines provide the means to better experience a relationship with God in Christ as a couple. Of course, the disciplines may be used by individuals, but my purpose is to take two individual followers of Christ and show them how to become one spiritually.

Allow me to introduce a sailing metaphor, which I will develop more in the next chapter. As individuals, you two compare to seaworthy monohull vessels. By these disciplines, I pray your two monohulls will be transformed into a catamaran! Have you seen those multihulled sailing vessels? They look a bit odd because we've been conditioned to think of boats as monohulls, like a ski boat or a Jon boat. When you see a catamaran, the picture kind of takes your breath away. It's broad and stable; it carries more passengers. You can travel quite quickly on its twin hulls.

Can you apply this metaphor to your marriage? You are two people, but one family. The catamaran sails on two hulls but is one boat.

Let's imagine these disciplines to be God's grace-tools to refit your two-vessel relationship into a twin-hulled marriage, with all the benefits! I'm excited to hear how the reconstruction goes because there are great benefits from the refit. That's what awaits us in the next chapter.

CHAPTER 4:

Like a Catamaran at Sea

Before reconstruction commences, let's look further at the value of catamaran spirituality. The disciplines become God's tools to refit your two boats into a new vessel. We will visit them shortly, but first, let's take a closer look at the changes and benefits awaiting you as God brings you together in His Spirit.

Catamaran Spirituality

Now we return to the catamaran metaphor of the last chapter. Picture you and your spouse as individual monohulled crafts being refitted into a sleek, twin-hulled catamaran. We're describing the life God intended for you emotionally, physically, and spiritually. We see two hulls joined into one vessel, catching the wind together, traveling in the same direction together, weathering the rough seas together, reaching forward together, and bearing more cargo together. Do you see why the catamaran offers a fitting picture of the couple becoming one spiritually?

Catamaran Advantages versus Monohulls

The catamaran (cat) bests the monohulled boat in the following ways:

- Sailing level: they don't "heel" over sideways nearly as much as the monohull.
- Speed: they can sail 25 to 30 percent faster.
- Safety: the cat proves almost impossible to turn over, and even less likely to sink.
- Space: the cat provides much more passenger, crew, and cargo space than the single-hulled sailboat.
- Maneuverability: the cat usually has two propellers, spread wide apart, which makes for much easier maneuvering in tight spots.

Each of these advantages also speak of the benefits to a couple when they refit their spiritual life into a twin-hulled craft. For example:

- They don't heel (lean over) as much: the catamaran couple doesn't find themselves pushed over by the winds of life as frequently. A heeling vessel may be in danger of capsizing. It also runs less efficiently and more slowly. Keeping both hulls in the water makes the couple's life run level, like the catamaran.

- They progress faster: the spiritual physics shows that when spouses pull together with the Lord's help, they travel farther and faster than if they pulled separately.
- They experience increased spiritual safety: the couple has each other's back spiritually speaking, especially as they pray for one another.
- The cat couple can bear a more significant cargo: the united couple may carry more burdens, offer more help, and provide better kingdom service than either one individually.
- The cat couple performs better: for example, musician Mary Beth often inspired the congregation with her piano, organ, or vocal offerings just before I stood to preach. Hearts were much more prepared for the words I brought because of the music she presented.

All our lives, we've heard that "two heads are better than one." Spiritually speaking, two hearts are better than one!

The Transformation

Now envision your marriage transitioning from two monohulls into a catamaran spirituality. Doesn't it sound appealing? Sure it does, because God intended it. As we envision the possibility, our hearts become possessed by the desire to realize it. I hope you sense that desire. I suggest that your new picture represents God's gentle, benevolent mastery over your hearts. You feel no manipulation; you don't see a hint of violence or violation. You are being wooed by God, the Holy Spirit, into a more fulfilling marriage. God is leading you to greater fulfillment in closeness as a couple, greater fulfillment together in nearness to God, and greater fulfillment as a team in kingdom usefulness.

Removing the Distance

Can you begin to see the marriage possibilities as you two grow together in your spiritual life? First, the solo sailing ends. The curses of the spiritually separated life most couples experience bear the marks of boredom and loneliness. Our distracted lives and disjointed spirituality sets us, as a couple, sailing different vessels on the same sea. At first, we keep our sailboats running side-by-side. Distance develops slowly and over time. One day, we look up to realize that we sail alone, our spouse barely in sight.

Catamaran spirituality prevents separated and disjointed couples. Life cannot become lonely or too burdensome when the Spirit empowers you and your spouse to travel together every nautical mile.

Facing the Challenges Confidently

Think how much more confidently you could meet the challenges of life if you two were strengthened by an engaged couple's devotional life. What if you bolstered your relationship by steeping your minds in Scripture, connecting with God's will through your prayers, and touching others' lives with God's love by your sacrificial service. Furthermore, picture the difference in your lives as you shift from self-protection to generosity, and when you live gratefully. This way, you find no challenge will capsize your marriage!

Seeing the Path

Once your minds begin to pick up the patterns revealed in the Bible, you see a glimmer of God's direction for your life. You read together about Abraham's life and begin to see what it means to live by faith. You read of King David's experiences and better understand how to trust in times of danger. Paul's travels, recorded in Acts, cause you to grasp the Holy Spirit's work in and through someone. The cat couple becomes adept at navigating by the stars hung in the biblical sky, book-by-book.

Realizing the Satisfaction and Joy

You begin to plug-in to God's will as you understand how God wishes to use you. You experience a deep level of satisfaction and steadfast joy. The most profound sense of fulfillment and the promise of abiding joy come from serving together.

When the two of you begin to follow your Lord into service, you may enter tentatively at first. You find that those initial service experiences offer better-than-expected returns on the energy investment. When that happens, you want more!

Spiritual Intimacy, the Last Great Marriage Frontier?

A catamaran spirituality offers each other benefits that add up to deepening spiritual intimacy. God intended for you and your companion to be welded together in love. Most people believe that feelings provide the bond. But we learn through the attempt to bond through feelings that the joint proves weak. Why? Because our emotions ebb and flow. Feelings depend too much on circumstances beyond our control. Do we wish to base our lives on fluctuating emotions? As one philosophy professor and ordained minister, Dallas Willard, once said, "Feelings are wonderful servants, but terrible masters!"

Of course, great sex supposedly cures all relational ills. But it doesn't take long to realize that's a big lie! In truth, a good sex life issues from a great relationship. If the couple shares antipathy, how will they share great sex? A mediocre relationship usually produces infrequent physical intimacy, without the fireworks and without the afterglow.

Instead, consider spiritual intimacy. Our spirit represents the deepest part of our being. When a couple shares transparently and vulnerably their deepest being, trust builds between the woman and man. As they approach God together in that early Eden-like state of trusting God, their creator applies grace to that trust. It's like welding; God puts high heat (grace) to the two spirits (faith), causing a fusion of lives. Now we're talking about a bond that will survive all kinds of life's pressures.

Adventures "at Sea"

Catamaran spirituality offers to take you into previously uncharted waters. God can direct your life into a love for Him and each other and to experiences of service you never dreamt you'd know. God plans for you two to become extraordinary examples of His love. God carries faithful couples on His path to reclaim and recreate the world. We get to be part of God's eternal plan. What an adventure; what a rush!

Spiritual Oxytocin

Have you heard about the "love hormone," named oxytocin? Amazingly, God created the hypothalamus to generate this hormone that, among other things, plays a prominent role in social bonding. Well, catamaran spirituality offers a regular shot of "spiritual oxytocin" into your marriage. Your experience of God's grace together bonds you to your spouse and to your heavenly Father.

One fact about oxytocin applies to one's spiritual life. You see, once the hypothalamus releases the hormone into the body, a part remains in the brain to stimulate the production of more oxytocin. Likewise, when a spiritual experience, like meaningful couple worship, watching a couple's service touch a life profoundly, or seeing the practice of generosity change someone's day, the spirit experiences a release of this "spiritual oxytocin." The spiritual bond in marriage strengthens, spiritual intimacy increases, and the practice of Spiritual Disciplines creates a stronger desire for further training.

Your life together may look nothing like this picture. In fact, you may doubt that you could ever realize such an experience together—but stop. Just pause and take a breath.

Results like these cannot be attained by the couple alone. Spiritual refitting cannot be done by the ship, but by the shipbuilder! If you submit together to God, then you give Him permission to transform you both.

How do I submit, you may wonder? Allow me to borrow a term Paul used in Ephesians 5:21-24 for the answer. As Paul applied his teaching to the first-century family, he employed a military term to encourage spouses' mutual submission. The word translated as "submit" literally means "to order under." Spouses were challenged to order-under each other voluntarily as they chose to order-under Jesus Christ. As I say to couples, the best way to lift each other up in Christ involves forgetting yourself long enough to stand beneath your spouse.

Admittedly, such self-forgetfulness feels unnatural because our natural attitude seeks a place above others, not beneath them. Yet with the help of God's abiding Spirit, we may do as Jesus challenged his would-be followers. In Luke 9:23, Jesus called those in earshot to deny the self (be selfless), take up the cross daily (in marriage, to shoulder God's purpose for your mate with God's help), and follow (through).

Ordering under each other as we order under Jesus Christ defines submission. Practicing a Spiritual Discipline expresses a powerful act of surrender, so keep that in mind as we move into the six Spiritual Disciplines.

Your ship has arrived. It's a beautiful, sleek, and stable catamaran. On it, God can navigate you safely through the roughest seas.

CHAPTER 5:

The Awe-Full Life – Worship

To commence construction on your catamaran spirituality, we turn first to worship. Why? The reason may surprise you. We need to change your focus to weld your lives together as one in Christ for others' sake. Worship lifts the human focus off us and our circumstances and up to God. Worship can be split into three settings for our purposes: individually, as a couple, and as a congregation. As an individual, you and I worship as we keep our focus on God throughout the day. As a couple, spouses worship as they lift their focus to God in gratitude for His presence, provision, and protection. Believers gather regularly to lift their focus to

God. They engage with God and each other through acts such as prayer, reading/hearing Scripture, singing songs, listening to teachings, sharing resources, and giving to those in need.

Notice that the individual and couple worship examples encompass a whole day, not just a few minutes in one day. The classic devotional time spent by an individual or a couple launches the day in a Godward direction. God sets the direction and trajectory. That is to imply that worship is a lifestyle. The worship we begin as a couple finds completion in all that we do throughout the day. It affects our attitude and actions, first toward spouse and family, then toward colleagues and neighbors, finally toward acquaintances and strangers. Each relationship ideally serves as a relational stage to act out our devotion toward God.

As worship applies to marriage, it provides couples with a means to accomplish Jesus' instruction, recorded in Luke 9:23, NIV: "Whoever wants to be my disciple must deny themselves and take up their cross daily and follow me." Through worship together, a couple shares and supports each other in the self-denial in preparation for selfless living. Therefore, worship stands as the first step in welding two lives together in Christ. Let the construction begin!

Worship's Essence

The essence of worship is reverence. When Jesus taught his disciples to pray, he began the model prayer with the heart of worship. Jesus taught them to pray first with adoration, as Matthew 6:9, KJV, demonstrates: "Our Father, which art in heaven, hallowed be thy name . . ."

Let's unwrap that present. Jesus begins with the less formal, more loving Aramaic word for father—Abba. The best English translation is not "father" but "daddy." In those times, a child, happy to see his father, would address him lovingly and respectfully as Abba.

We may assume that Jesus encouraged his brothers to enter God's presence expecting to be received as a beloved child. If we address Him as Abba, then we approach a loving daddy with humble, happy respect.

The next phrase, "who art in heaven," places God literally in the "heavens," or the expanse above. You could envision a white-bearded man with gleaming robes of light seated on a throne above us. As children, we probably pictured God this way.

Jesus sought to speak of God's separateness. Heaven here captures more of God's superiority, morally, powerfully, and mercifully. In the Hebrew and Greek languages, the words for "holy" meant separate, or to be set apart. Jesus reminds us of God's holiness. Forgive the play on words, but we humans tend to lose sight of the invisible God. Life distracts, whether you are a first-century fisherman or twenty-first-century IT consultant. We forget God's greatness, splendor, mercy, and love for us. Jesus calls us to worship by remembering God's dazzling magnificence. To recapture that vision enraptures the soul. Worship begins here!

The final clause uses one term and one idea that deserves a closer look. Since the word to "hallow" comes from Old English, I consulted the online Cambridge Dictionary. To hallow means "to give something great importance or respect." It speaks of offering admiration and respect; to hallow someone means you revere the person. To hallow God means to show reverence toward God; it means acknowledging God's great importance to you. What exactly do you hallow?

The phrase "thy name" changed meanings since Jesus' day. The twenty-first-century mind thinks of a person's designation. Instead, Jesus' hearers understood that God's spirit and character deserved reverence.

In that time, a name often contained information about the person's being and character. In fact some familiar biblical names, like Immanuel, which means "God with us," carried valuable freight for the hearers. It bore an eternal promise!

Today parents often choose a name for its euphony, its uniqueness, or because it represents a family member. For example, both of my grandsons carry part of my name; the older bears my middle name, Dean, and my younger grandson was given my first name, William, and is called Liam.

Giving someone a family name may most approximate the biblical era's practice, hoping that the family member's life and character transfers to the younger member. To reverence God's name amounts to respecting God's being and character. Worship of God remembers and reverences His divinely different being and nature as the new or renewed focus of a couple's marriage. We couples-in-Christ seek a relationship with our Creator God through the Redeemer Son by the transforming Spirit's help.

Do you now understand why worship stands as first among Spiritual Discipline equals? The process for welding a couple's two lives into one unit in Christ for others begins and ends with a focus on our Creator who recreates us in Christ by the Spirit.

Stand in Awe

To take the idea of reverential worship a bit further, we see that reverence comes from a Latin word that means "to stand in awe." The posture of worship must be awe-full.

You've had these kinds of moments, haven't you? Those human experiences of awe help us understand the experience of worship. Did you ever stand at the rim of the Grand Canyon? Have you stood in the shadow of the pyramids of Giza? Maybe you've risen early on vacation to catch a glorious sunrise over the ocean, or sat still to drink in a sunset viewed from a mountain perch? I have felt deep awe from my morning devotional spot, like a cardinal in the crepe myrtle or low clouds hugging mountain tops. On occasion, a trackless blanket of snow speaks to me of newness and renewal. Haven't we all been gripped by awe as we held a newborn, so innocent and full of unrealized potential?

What's common in each moment of awe? Each one grants us a different perspective from which to see life. The sense of greatness causes us to feel overwhelmed, humbled, or small. Still, awe breaks through our limited perspective with a breathtaking moment. We don't see life the same in that awe-filled moment. When we stand in awe, we approach the place where the veil between heaven and earth, Creator and creature is thinnest. We see what we have missed; we know what we had forgotten. We sense reality that lies just beyond our fingertips' reach.

Awe and reverence occur when we press life's pause button and still our bodies and minds so we can see God from a different perspective: a breathtaking moment when, through the veil, we catch a glimpse of our Creator, Redeemer, and Transformer. We need these moments regularly because we live at a pace that typically does not allow us the luxury of stopping to remember and revere God. If not built into life, when do we stand humbly in awe of the Eternal One? How often do we allow God to grace us with a new perspective on life? If your life resembles mine, such times are probably rare.

Worship, therefore, describes the act of standing in awe of God, which leads to respect, dependence, praise, and gratitude for our Father in heaven. When we experience that awe-full moment, we see our lives anew in His light, through His intention, and with divine purpose.

Response!

Worship finds completion as we respond humbly to God's presence. Authentic worship must give an expression of that awe and reverence of God in some action. Worship that remains abstract lacks completion, as an artist's preliminary sketch lacks the pigment that makes it a painting.

Worship may not be limited to an act. Worship is more of a lifestyle, not just an event on the weekly calendar or occasional reverential moment. The Westminster Shorter Catechism (1646 and 1647) begins by asking the catechumen, "What is the chief end of man?" The correct answer is, "Man's chief end is to glorify God, and to enjoy him forever." This sounds like worship to me, doesn't it to you?

Here's this discipline's goal: getting you as a couple to live in awe-full response to your God. Your worship transforms your perspective on everything and imbues your days with eternal purpose and divine passion. Your purpose and passion find expression in kingdom service beside each other as you cooperate with God's will. In worship, you receive His love toward you, then complete the worship act by allowing that love to flow through you to others. You find forgiveness before God in worship, but you cannot contain that mercy and grace. You extend forgiveness to one who hurt or offended you. You come to see life as a gift as you worship your Creator. All that defines you, from personality to possession, issued from God's generous hand. Now you sense that He gave you these gifts to share, not hoard. You begin sharing your life and goods with those around you. Worship finds completion!

In the devotionals you do for this discipline, keep in mind the awe-full experience is genuine when it leads to action. As you grow together, you desire to translate that awe, respect, and reverence into service. At worship's best, we witness God using our reverential actions to lead others to the thin veil that they may also worship. Your worship finds its perfection.

✝ WORSHIP DEVOTIONAL STARTERS

I suggest the following to those who do not have a couple's devotional life. First, find a quiet place to read, discuss, and write. Location counts heavily in a meaningful devotional life. Find a place with few distractions and meet

God there frequently. After a while, you will find that your body and mind will begin to shift into a worshipful mode as you enter. Make it a comfortable space for you both. Good lighting serves the eyes and is a metaphor for being in God's presence. A Bible you understand (preferably a study Bible) will become the centerpiece of your devotional life together. Keep a pen, paper, and markers handy. I found gel highlighters work well and do not bleed through Bible pages.

Now if you've never developed an individual devotional life, I recommend baby steps. Don't begin by filling twenty minutes of devotional time. Five to ten minutes, in the beginning, will be adequate. Relax and don't set lofty goals at first. After a few weeks of seven-minute devotional times together, you may wish to add a minute or two with readings from a devotional book. For Mary Beth and me, the discussions flowed freer after a while.

Get started, be consistent, and allow God to develop your bond. If you miss a day or two because of events beyond your control, be at peace. Just move back to your couple's devotionals as soon as you can.

Now you understand that worship provides a God-centric refocusing of your lives, the first step toward togetherness in Christ. Together you approach your heavenly Daddy, who loves you with an everlasting love. You respond to His invitation for a relationship by moving respectfully and reverently into His presence.

Instead of a shivering fear, you "come into His presence with thanksgiving and into His courts with praise" (Ps. 100:4, paraphrased KJV). As your couple's devotional life develops, you find it marked by joy in His presence.

May your Bible reading together lead you to worship.

Bible Reading Structure

Here's my recommendation for those with little devotional experience. You may apply these four Ps to each of the passages you choose:

- Passage: Read the passages over a couple of times.
- Past: What did the passages say to the original hearers/readers?
- Present: What caught my attention in the passages? Share with your spouse.
- Prayer: Turn the thoughts impressed on you by God's abiding Spirit into a prayer.

Allow me to illustrate with a devotional that Mary Beth and I would have. We have considered Proverbs 3:5-6 numerous times. The NIV reads: "Trust in the Lord with all your heart and lean not on your own understanding; in all your ways acknowledge him, and he will make your paths straight."

We understand that Solomon offered this tidbit of wisdom in the context of a more extended section on the nature and benefits of wisdom. The essential teaching of this section reveals wisdom as a life lived in the right relationship with God. The popular definition may describe wisdom as the accumulation of experience that shapes decisions, but not so in the Proverbs. Solomon understood that wisdom issues from the Lord (Prov. 9:10: "The fear of the Lord is the beginning of wisdom . . ."). Based on that understanding of wisdom, a person in Solomon's day who trusted in and acknowledged God would benefit from God's guidance. His path would be made straight.

The present application of Proverbs 3:5-6 steers us away from our natural inclination to "lean on our own understanding" in favor of whole-heartedly trusting God's leadership. For example, take the last few months of 2016 when I faced the decision to retire or remain as pastor. Thirty-eight years of service conditioned me to stay in the shepherd's role. Friends encouraged me to stay. Mary Beth and I turned to God in private worship. Within days, I clearly heard God directing me to step out of that role, against my conditioned inclination and our friends' encouragement.

We turned that inkling of thought into a prayer: "Father, if you would have me retire, then confirm it for both Mary Beth and me." The confirmation did not strike like a bolt of lightning. Instead, God granted us an unusual calm in what promised to be an unsettling decision. Several years hence, we continue to witness God's guidance on this new path!

I strongly suggest that you keep a record of your daily devotionals, note the passage, the original message, the message to yourself, and the prayer arising from the present application. I have returned to the notes of those days and that decision on several occasions. Each reading reminds how God led us through that difficult decision with renewed strength and determination to trust and follow.

If you need a nudge into your "P-patch," consider some of the following passages. Many of them are considered classic passages of worship.

- Isaiah 6:1-6: Isaiah experiences an extraordinary moment of worship during his regular rounds as an on-duty priest in the Temple.
- Mark 9:2-4: Jesus allows Peter, James, and John to witness an extraordinary event that moved them.
- John 20:24-29: Thomas only believes and worships after he touches the risen Jesus.
- Habakkuk 3:17-19: The prophet makes a profound statement of worship in the face of need.
- Amos 5:21-24: Amos delivers a stern word about authentic and inauthentic worship.
- Psalm 8:1-9: David's worship set to verse demonstrates how creation may lead us to the thin veil.
- Psalm 11:4: David worships under the searching eye of God.

- Psalm 51:16-17: David leaves a legacy of his profound worship in the wake of his moral and spiritual failure.
- Exodus 3:1-6: Moses finds God on the backside of nowhere, and his life and direction are changed.
- Psalm 96:1-3, 9: The nameless psalmists call the nations to praise God with trembling (reverence).

Worship Completed

As you read and discussed the passages, what did the Spirit nudge you to do in response to God? Make a note of those "nudgings" and what actions you took together due to your joint worship.

CHAPTER 6:

What's God's Will for Us? – Bible Reading

While worship stands as first among equals in the disciplines, as you read in the last chapter, profound worship involves God revealing Himself, which He does best through sacred Scripture. The Bible serves as God's divinely inspired revelation of Himself and His purposes. As such, the Bible serves as the cornerstone of most disciplines. The Bible ranks as the number one resource for us as Christians.

Build on the Solid Foundation

Through Scripture, we understand who God is and how He reaches out to us. God intended the Bible to be a revelation of His working in, among, and through humans. What other book compares?

The Bible contains sixty-six separate books and was written by over forty different authors. Among its diverse authors, we find kings, prophets, priests, fishermen, a tax collector, and a doctor. While most of the Bible books were written in and around Israel, parts of Jeremiah were penned in Africa, and other books were composed in Europe. To complete all sixty-six books of the Bible, it took over 1500 years!

The Bible tops the bestseller list every year. Estimates put Bible sales at over five billion copies. Annually, Bible purchases amount to over half a billion dollars.

The message of the Bible continues to inspire readers. Why? From a faith stance, we believe God inspired the writing and the preservation of the Bible to reveal His desire for a close and eternal relationship with His creatures. Therefore, when you read the Scripture, understand God's desire to connect with us through each book.

We build our relationship with God on the book He provided—the record that focuses on the divine-human relationship. Every Spiritual Discipline serves an essential purpose, but reading and understanding the Bible ranks as first among equals. The Bible teaches us how far God has gone to reestablish a relationship with us. It reveals how to live in the right relationship with Him and each other. Through it, God comforts us with glimpses of eternal life with Him, and warns us with glimpses of eternal life separated from Him.

No wonder we set the Bible as the foundation for a steady spiritual life together with Him.

A Love Story, Not a Rule Book

When the reader maintains a proper perspective in Bible reading, the message of good news shines through as a love story. Many approach the Bible as a rule book. These readers take only parts of Scripture, like the Ten Commandments, and perceive the Bible as a book of dos and don'ts.

Suppose you read only parts of the Bible out of their context, like the Ten Commandments and several chapters in Leviticus. In that case, you might fall victim to a misunderstanding of the Bible's purpose. The dos and don'ts become regulations to be kept as a requisite for relationship. Read properly, God's commands express how one is to behave because they stand in the right relationship with God, not to *earn* a right relationship with Him. Therefore, the dos and don'ts we read in the Bible serve to enhance the understanding of our relationship with Him.

Developing Our Hearing

Since we wish to understand this divine-human relationship thoroughly, we read and study Scripture.

Steeping the mind in Scripture cultivates "ears" to hear His voice, both inside and outside the Bible. Just as we bathe tea bags in hot water so that the tea's flavor permeates the water, we infuse our minds in Scripture so that God's "flavor" can permeate our life.

We want to be colored by God's abiding presence. By listening daily to the words of the Bible, our understanding picks up on the themes of love, repentance, forgiveness, reconciliation, salvation, and sanctification, to name a few. As we become more familiar with how God related to the Bible's characters, we see how God relates to us.

Our "hearing" sharpens. We pick up God's whispered tones beyond the Bible. We hear the call to forgive when we have been wronged. Imagine how that will revolutionize your marriage! What if your understanding of God's place in your life moves you to ask for or grant forgiveness? Spiritual intimacy in your marriage remains intact because the disturbance in the relationship was short-lived.

The purpose of all Spiritual Disciplines revolves around attaining and maintaining closeness and dependence on our heavenly Father. A steady diet of Bible reading and study will serve to strengthen your spiritual life; it will allow you to better see how God works in your life so you can cooperate. It shapes your relationship by forging your understanding of God's purpose for marriage. Bible study also allows you to make the most of the other Spiritual Disciplines.

If you hadn't thought about the Bible's importance in a couple's life, can you now see its value? The Bible stands as God's greatest support for a couple's spiritual life.

Two Reasons We Read the Bible

First, we read the Bible for information. Information gathering acts as stage one in a couple's or individual's devotional life. For new believers, or those just beginning to grow spiritually, information is critical. How else are we to cooperate with God as He transforms us if we don't understand God's goals? For example, how do we cooperate with God's desire to spend time with Him if we haven't read passages like Psalm 46:10, NIV: "Be still and know that I am God"? As we meditate on this passage and discuss it with our spouse, we allow the Spirit to shape our thinking and desire. God wants us to spend time with Him, and we realize a growing craving to spend time with God. We cooperate, and progress accelerates. That leads to the second reason to read the Bible.

Second, we read for transformation or spiritual formation. You may ask, what exactly is spiritual formation? I like the definition offered by M. Robert Mulholland in his book *Invitation to a Journey*. On page 15, Mulholland defines spiritual formation as "a process of being conformed to the image of Christ for the sake of others." Apply his definition to transformational Bible reading. To resemble Jesus, who gave His life to benefit others, we allow God's Spirit to use Scripture to form our lives. I suggest our beloved as the primary "other" whom God intends to affect through us.

Consequently, transformation is the ultimate goal of reading and discussing the Bible together. At the beginning of the spiritual journey together, our individual lives do not yet reflect God's character. Neither can our marriage reflect God's love for each other. We cannot maximize our union with God's purpose and passion until we understand His purpose and passion for us.

To strengthen that understanding, we read, discuss, and apply our learning from Scripture. During our attempts, the Spirit leads and empowers. Our effort, and the Spirit's energy, create transformation into Christ-likeness—over time.

Once more, hear this encouragement: spiritual formation for individuals and couples is a process of being conformed to the image of Christ for the sake of others. So transformation takes our effort, plus the Spirit's energy, over time. God puts the two of us in the Spirit's Crock-Pot to cook slowly until the old, tough lives become tender. Don't rush the process but trust the chef!

Check Your Sword

Do you remember how Paul used a sword as a metaphor for the Scripture? You'll find it in Ephesians 6:17 and alluded to in Hebrews 4:12-13. Before you embark on this couple's journey, check your sword. What Bible do you have? We live in a blessed era when scholarship makes many versions of Scripture available to us. The version you use needs to "fit" you.

Many people have an old King James version lying around the house. The KJV reads poetically in many areas, especially in the Psalms. But it uses the common language of the seventeenth-century Englishman. The translation done by the forty-seven scholars King James assembled produced a version of the Bible in Elizabethan English. Even though beautiful in its day, all language remains dynamic. English usage changed in the intervening four centuries, making idioms lost to twenty-first-century readers. For example, in Galatians 1:13, KJV, we read: "For ye have heard of my conversation in time past in the Jews' religion, how that beyond measure I persecuted the church of God." In the seventeenth century, the word "conversation" meant something different from today. Now read the New International Version (NIV) as a modern example: "For you have heard of my previous way of life in Judaism, how intensely I persecuted the church of God." Makes more sense to our twenty-first-century ears, right?

Enter a variety of newer translations. Some of those translations sought to stay as close to the original languages of the Bible as possible. The committee of scholars sought a word-for-word translation as often as possible, but they sometimes found the old idioms challenging to capture with contemporary English. In those cases, they remained as true to the original expressions as our language would allow. If you wish to have a version like this, check out the New American Standard version (NAS).

Other translations sought a thought-for-thought translation. These scholars meant to capture the original language's thoughts and translate them into our contemporary language to function the same way for the reader. The Contemporary English Version (CEV) represents this thought-for-thought translation.

Other versions attempted to blend the word-for-word accuracy with the thought-for-thought clarity. The New International Version and the New Living Translation (NLT) fit in this category. I happen to use the NIV most often, while my bride mostly uses the NLT. However, we both consult other translations to see the nuances of language brought out by each scholarly team.

If you don't have a Bible, or if you're in the market for a new one, you can check out these other versions online or at your local bookstore. Find a translation that makes the most sense to you. Choose several poignant or well-known passages, like Psalm 23, Genesis 1, and Matthew 5, and read them in different translations; choose the one that fits you best.

Before you take off to the bookstore, let me make one more suggestion.

Get a Study Bible

You will benefit greatly from owning at least one study Bible. Generally, a study Bible will have an introduction to each book that gives vital information for deeper understanding and an outline of the book. You'll also find comments that provide information or explanations of unfamiliar items at the bottom of each page. For example, in Matthew 19:3, certain Pharisees sought to test Jesus with a divorce question: "Is it lawful for a man to divorce his wife for any and every reason?" The notes below that passage in my NIV Study Bible explained the nuance of their question.

They alluded to two interpretations of Deuteronomy 24:1-4, the schools of Shammai and Hillel. Rabbi Shammai adherents held a very limited understanding of divorce. The more liberal Hillel's camp taught that a husband could divorce his wife for any reason.

Some study Bibles add the explanatory notes along with the text. The Voice Translation places the explanations in the body of the chapter. Many study Bibles also include sidebars that give specific information about something in the passage. You may find an explanation about a unit of measurement, like "stadia" as a measure of distance, or some mention of currency, like a "shekel weight" of silver.

Many of the better versions offer study Bibles. In our home, we possess study Bibles in the New International Version, the Revised Standard and New Revised Standard

Versions, the New King James Version, the New Living Translation, and The Voice Translation. I highly recommend that couples use a study Bible. They cost more, but they give value beyond the Bible's price.

Preparing Your Heart and Mind

So far I've suggested that you prepare by finding a quiet place to read together. I've also recommended that you have a modern translation study Bible. Perhaps the most critical step to meaningful Bible reading as a couple involves a brief prayer at the start of each session. Simply hold hands and confess your need for the Spirit's presence as you open the Bible for transformation.

The prayer need not be long, only genuine. The Bible will read like a sterile book without the Spirit's illumination. Many university classes read the Bible as literature; approaching the Bible with our intelligence alone renders the reading an exercise in studying literature. God wants you to experience His presence. God desires to transform you individually and as a couple through this Spirit-illuminated study.

Use the opening prayer to open your minds and hearts to God's transforming presence. You and your spouse may alternate praying, or you can both offer a prayer of preparation. At first, I prayed. Mary Beth still felt unsure of herself. The longer we have shared together, the more Mary Beth prays. We often pray during the same prayer.

If I mention someone in my prayer, she often adds her prayers for that person too. My heart soars when I hear her loving, compassionate prayers! I'm so glad we now share devotional times together.

Understanding this New Vessel

Moving from a monohulled sailboat to a larger catamaran requires adjustment. Likewise, expect your Bible reading together to feel a bit awkward at first. The more you two exercise this discipline, the more comfortable you'll become. Trust that God wants to strengthen your marriage with this bond and will help you discipline yourselves to seek Him with this time. He's welding you into a dual-hulled vessel to sail together through this life and into the next.

 BIBLE READING DEVOTIONAL

With a study Bible in hand, a quiet place, and minds and hearts prepared, you're ready to practice this discipline. Don't forget to do the following with each passage you choose:

- Passage: Read the passage over a couple of times.
- Past: What did the passage say to the original hearers/readers?

- Present: What caught my attention in the passage? Share with your spouse.
- Prayer: Turn the thoughts impressed on you by God's abiding Spirit into a prayer.

Keep a record of your daily devotionals; note the passage, the original message, the message to you, and the prayer arising from the present application.

- Psalm 119:103-105: As God uses the Scripture to light your way, your "taste" for devotional reading grows as the appetite for pure honey.
- Psalm 119:10-12: Consider the benefit of memorizing scripture.
- 1 Peter 2:2-3: May we crave the life-giving milk!
- Isaiah 40:8: God's Word remains when all else fades.
- Deuteronomy 8:3: Jesus quoted this passage from memory when tempted by the devil in the wilderness.
- Proverbs 2:1-6: Seek the wisdom of God's words.
- Isaiah 55:10-11: God assures Israel through Isaiah that His words have purpose and power that will not be denied.
- Psalm 19:7-11: Reflect on this encouraging summary of the Scripture's value in life.

- 2 Timothy 3:16-17: Paul outlines the benefits of Scripture for the believer (and couple!).
- Hebrews 4:12: The author recounts the decisive power of the illuminated Scripture.

Bible Reading: Engaging Mind and Heart

How did the Bible reading together go? Did you find the water smooth or choppy? Most importantly, how did God speak to you as a couple through the readings? What actions have you taken because of this activity?

As God reveals Himself to you through Scripture, you find both mind and heart engaged. Paul hinted at this to the Roman believers in Romans 12:2, KJV: "Do not be conformed to this world but be transformed by the renewing of your mind . . . ." Our transformation into Christlikeness begins in the mind. From there, God's Spirit regenerates the believer's heart and behavior into living like Jesus lived.

Remember, the disciplines "cook" at Crock-Pot speed! The changes God makes in you may seem very slow. I've come to see that as the deliberate plan of God. We learn over time to depend on God totally and to love Him "with all our heart" (Matt. 22:34-40). Be patient, or better put, give the Spirit of God more time to accommodate you to this discipline.

I'd like to share a bit of wisdom a friend shared with me decades ago for living in a success-oriented, hard-driving culture that values winning and accumulating over relationships. He said to me: "It's not how much of the Bible you get through, it's how much of the Bible gets through you." Chew on that.

CHAPTER 7:

Learning to Listen – Prayer

Let's assume our couple worship locks our gaze on God. Then let's say the Spirit uses our Bible reading and study to engage our minds and hearts in Christ-mirroring transformation. Next we add the discipline of prayer.

Wait! When you read the word *prayer*, you may envision something different from the discipline of prayer. Sadly, most praying is reduced to "grocery-list praying" and "foxhole bargaining."

As a couple, you will discover the discipline of prayer to be a much richer dialogue. It's fair to say the exchange does not look like a two-way street, both sides being equal in length and width. Instead, as you two grow in this discipline, the thoroughfare of prayer may seem more like a four-lane highway on God's side and a single-lane road on yours.

What Is Prayer?

Let's look at a much more satisfying and effectual discipline of listening prayer. Philip Yancy hints at the difference with this comment: "Prayer is the act of seeing reality from God's point of view."[3]

Some say that prayer is a conversation with God, and while that's true to a point, it's like saying Michael Jordan was a basketball player or the *Mona Lisa* is a painting or that *Gone with the Wind* is a movie. While each statement is true, we also know that Michael Jordan was arguably the best professional basketball player ever. We know that the *Mona Lisa* is the most recognizable portrait painting of all time. As for movies, did you know that the receipts of *Gone with the Wind*, when adjusted for inflation, make it the number-one grossing movie ever? In truth, we may define prayer as a conversation with God, but it's so much more! At its depth, prayer describes a relationship with God. More significant still, prayer describes a relationship with God that God initiates.

---

3   Philip Yancy, *Prayer: Does It Make any Difference* (Grand Rapids, MI: Zondervan, 2016), 29.

Unique Communication

When we pray, we communicate as an inferior to a superior. Modern sensibilities struggle with anything less than equality. Can we count ourselves equal with God? No, but when we consider the miracle of prayer, this over-under relationship becomes earth-shaking because we believe God wants a conversation with us and maintains a primary purpose for this communication. In prayer, our heavenly Father invites us to cooperate in His activity to transform His world!

Why Pray?

When our prayers reach their God-given potential, we pray-ers align our thoughts with God's benevolent will. So many prayers begin with our wants—"give us," "show us," "lead us," or "heal us." All of these have a place and time, but not the first place or all the time.

Imagine you are a college student aiming toward an astronaut's career. Amazingly, someone knowing this offers you a private interview with Edwin "Buzz" Aldrin—wow, a private audience with one of the first men to walk on the moon! Though you may have a thousand questions, what does wisdom dictate? Yes, listen. You realize that your questions may interfere with Mr. Aldrin's telling you something you need to know, something you don't know to ask. He will likely answer most of your questions if you listen. After he shares his experience, you can still pose your remaining queries.

Listening first and asking questions later models the reality that you're focused on Mr. Aldrin in this conversation. You shift your focus off yourself and onto him as the center of the conversation. Likewise, in prayer, our listening disciplines us to change the locus from us to God as the center of the conversation.

How much more does listening figure into our conversation with God? Faith asserts that God has much to show and tell us. If we discipline ourselves to put God in the center of the prayer, we stand to learn more than when we focus on our wants, concerns, and perceived needs.

Hearing God

You wonder, "How can I hear God? I've never heard God speak!" Maybe you heard God, but you didn't recognize His voice.

Let me explain this statement by first considering the importance of nonverbal communication among humans. The percentage of verbal cues is less than half of all communication cues. Body language and tone of voice carry 60 to 90 percent of the communication freight. You hear words, but you also hear the tone of voice, see gestures, watch facial expressions, and note other cues, like blushing or flushing, that color how you understand the words.

I suggest that God's "nonverbal communication" says more than His words. In prayer, God's words likely fall below 1 percent of the communication. For example, I have found that God often communicates through gentle "nudges." A couple hears that a neighbor will have outpatient surgery, so they pray for that neighbor. Later that day, the wife has an idea to fix a meal for the family when he returns home from the hospital. That same day, the husband thinks about how their neighbor keeps his yard so well-manicured but will be laid up for a couple of weeks, so he decides to mow their lawn.

That evening the couple, not knowing each other's ideas, share what they want to do. At that moment, they realize it was more than coincidence. After praying for the neighbor, God nudged them with ideas that they accepted. God spoke to them.

My wife and I often share another experience of God speaking through the nudge with each other. One of us "hears" the name of a person bubble up in our thoughts often. Usually that person has not entered our thoughts or populated our conversation together for some time. Yet we sense the need to make contact.

Let me tell you about Tony's experience. I enjoy the good fortune of meeting with a group of Christian brothers at Chick-fil-A every Wednesday at 6 a.m., and one of those friends is Tony. One morning Tony shared with the group about a very distinct dream he had. He rarely remembers dreams, but this one stuck vividly. He dreamed about a woman he's known since childhood. She and her husband have served as missionaries for more than two decades in eastern Europe, but Tony had not talked with her for years. He couldn't shake the thought that something may be wrong.

Tony prayed about it, discussed it with his bride, and they agreed he should call. He did and inquired how she and her family were doing. After expressing surprise and gratitude for his call, the woman told Tony about several issues related to health and children. He hung up, convinced that God had nudged him to call and encourage and pray for his friends. *This* represents God's communication to us.

We have grown to see these events as more than random thoughts. Why? Because our contact—whether through a visit, text, email, or call like Tony's—often returns something like, "Wow, how did you know I needed that?" We may also hear something like, "What perfect timing for your call," or "I needed this visit and encouragement." We see these random thoughts now as God's timing and God's "voice."

On rare occasions, I have "heard" God speak. God interrupted my train of thought with clear messages—so clear that the idea seemed to shout at me.

I remember one such instance that occurred in September 2016 after I announced my retirement from the congregation I had served for twenty-three and a half years. Some gladly received that announcement, and many were sad to see us go. A few insisted that we remain for at least two more years. This idea became a written recommendation for the congregation to consider. To accept it would mean withdrawing my retirement notice.

I was torn, so I took the matter to God. For a couple of days I heard nothing. Then one morning, as I prayed about another issue, I heard this: "If you leave, I will do something new!" The words came so clearly, forcefully, and unexpectedly that I froze in my chair.

In a moment, I knew the answer to my prayer: continue with the retirement because it would be best for the congregation and for my family. The new pastor arrived on the field, the church seems to be healthy, and my bride and I feel confident in God's new direction. I'm now a marriage coach, which captures the two things I loved most about pastoring: teaching and working with couples and individuals to improve their lives in Christ.

Only a few times in my life have such divine communications broken through my thoughts and prayers. When they came, they always sounded like a brief statement. They came from right field, meaning that God voiced a thought not on my radar at that moment. These words consistently arrived with a profound effect on my spirit. The source of the idea has been unmistakable.

Even though these experiences stand out in my memory, I don't attempt to build my prayer life on these rare moments. While God occasionally uses words/thoughts to speak, He sometimes uses subtler means of grabbing my attention. I may feel the gentle nudge or the nearly silent whisper. Most often, inspired desires guide me in prayer.

When God speaks, in whatever manner, He communicates with a purpose.

Prayer's Purpose

As stated in the previous section, spiritual formation is the process of being conformed to Christ for others' sake. This assertion hints at the purpose of prayer captured by a Chinese believer, Watchman Nee: "Prayer is the union of the believer's thought with the will of God. The prayer which a believer utters on earth is but the voicing of the Lord's will in heaven."[4]

Prayer rests as another vital cornerstone of spiritual formation along with Bible reading/study. As we consider prayer's purpose, let's emphasize the last phrase of the spiritual formation process, "for the sake of others."

Prayer possesses many facets, including prayers for personal direction or healing or provision. The prayer diamond's table facet—the largest facet, which allows in the most light—would be the selfless facet.

---

4   Watchman Nee, *Let Us Pray* (Richmond, VA: Christian Fellowship Publishers, 1977), 3.

Hear the ultimate purpose for the believer's life phrased beautifully from Paul's letter to the Ephesians (2:8-10) in The Voice translation:

> For it's by God's grace that you have been saved. You receive it through faith. It was not our plan or our effort, but God's gift, pure and simple. You didn't earn it, not one of us did, so don't go around bragging that you must have done something amazing. For we are the product of His hand, heaven's poetry etched on lives, created in the Anointed, Jesus, to accomplish the good works God arranged long ago.

Notice verse 10 again: "For we are the product of His hand, heaven's poetry etched on lives, created in the Anointed, Jesus, to accomplish the good works God arranged long ago." God made us and filled us with His poetry to fulfill the good works established long beforehand for us to do. The Greek word translated here as "the product" is *poeme.* Seem familiar? Of course, we transliterate this work into English as "poem." Our lives in God's hands look like a beautiful poem, a masterpiece, crafted to communicate His eternal love. Our life-page bears the life-giving words of the Creator for all to read! This is a great purpose, right?

Jesus spoke of our purpose in Luke 9:23 (again using The Voice translation): "If any of you want to walk My path, you're going to have to deny yourself. You'll have to take up your cross every day and follow Me."

The cross remains the follower's purpose. We will not suffer crucifixion, but we accept the cross as God's purpose worked through our lives for others' sake.

Prayer may be considered the starting line for the spiritual marathon of life. God laid out a course for us, enables us to run it, and calls us to make this course the center of our lives.

You now run this course together. You become one of the primary enabling channels for your spouse. You deny yourself, seek to embody God's purpose for him/her every day, and follow through with the Spirit's help. Your prayers with, and for, your beloved figure significantly in God's plan for him or her. Prayer on behalf of your spouse becomes a selfless utterance of God's grace into your beloved's life. God uses your prayers to transform him/her into the complete-in-Christ child He already sees.

Let's connect the dots about how God uses your prayers:

- Prayer is a conversational lifestyle expressing a relationship with God.
- God has a purpose for this communication in relationships around you, starting with your spouse.

- Communication occurs superior to inferior so that listening becomes our primary human posture in prayer.
- As we listen, God nudges, impresses, changes desire, brings unexpected opportunity, raises to mind novel thoughts; in other words, God "speaks."
- We respond with trust and obedience.
- Our spouse remains our first prayer priority: we listen for God's direction for our beloved.

Think, then, of prayer this way:

Prayer works like a simple light circuit:

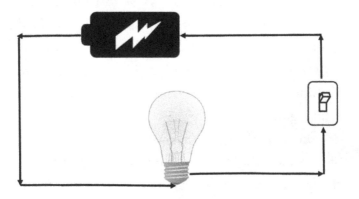

- God is the power source with wires (His connections) to you and to others.

- The light bulb represents the person(s) in whose life God intends to work.
- The switch is you, or you and your spouse, through whom God works.

You listen to God and sense the nudge, like a sudden concern for someone. You respond with a prayer for the one(s) concerning you, like texting, calling, or emailing your support. This obedient response closes the prayer circuit. The other person experiences a surge of divine power, like encouragement.

Prayer, as God intended, begins with seeking God's direction. Sadly, as I stated earlier, most praying is reduced to "grocery-list praying" and "foxhole bargaining." We all do it. In desperate moments we turn to God for help, and there is nothing wrong with that. I believe God hears those prayers, even if He doesn't always answer as we wish.

Once our understanding of prayer matures, we transition over time to seeking God's will first, then bringing our concerns afterward.

The remarkable transformation God effects in our life enables us to trust Him more, regardless of the circumstances. We come to experience His faithful provision and protection so that we fear less. Our prayer life changes. We start with God, putting others, including our spouse, before ourselves. Concerns for self fall to a humble third. A growing trust may reduce many problems to small requests, or even to an affirmation of trusting God to handle it—a once-larger fear now reduced to a trusting footnote in prayer. Your practice in listening prayer leads you to selflessly purposeful prayer.

Let's recap. God grants us the privilege of continual communication with Him. We count that continual communication as prayer. Initially, we often express self-focused prayers. Our prayers travel one way as requests from us to God. Over time we learn that God has the plan, not us. God is the focus of prayer, not us. God has more to say to us than we first thought. The Spirit helps us to realize the value of listening to God for direction. He often answers most of our questions or renders them unimportant if we spend more time listening than talking.

We realize along the way that God often prompts us, or nudges us, to pray for a specific person or to make a particular decision. We learn that when we respond to God's promptings, He often uses our prayers and actions as a blessing in someone else's life. God's purpose grows clearer in those moments so that we see ourselves as the "switches" He uses to channel His power to another. What changes God has in store for our prayer life together!

Notice the spiritual structure God is building discipline by discipline. Through worship, you two have your life-focus turned off of you and onto God. Worship grows from an occasional event into a living lifestyle of reverent relationship with God in Christ.

Bible reading and study engages your mind with the God of history who invites you into a deeper relationship. As you love birds respond to God's invitation, you grant His Spirit permission to transform you degree by degree into Christ's likeness (2 Cor. 2:18). Your relationship with God goes to new depths, and your relationship to each other reaches new heights.

As your focus locks onto heaven and your mind and heart experience more significant transformation, your prayers take on a new purpose. Your prayers move from more of a monologue, where you recite your needs and requests to God, and slowly move to dialogues, where you two learn to listen first and speak later. The disciplines have begun to enrich your relationship with God and each other!

How will God transform your couple prayers from grocery lists to light switches?

✝ PRAYER DEVOTIONAL STARTERS

It is time to practice the spiritual discipline of listening prayer. Consider the following passages as starting points for listening to God. This puts emphasis on step three, the present application of the passage. What will God "say" to you? How will God "nudge" you to selfless service of your spouse first and then others? Here's a reminder of the simple four-step suggestion for this exercise:

- Passage: Read the passage over a couple of times.
- Past: What did the passage say to the original hearers/readers?
- Present: What caught my attention in the passage? Share with your spouse.
- Prayer: Turn the thoughts impressed on you by God's abiding Spirit into a prayer.

Are you keeping a record of your daily devotionals? What actions do you feel impelled to take because of your devotionals together?

- Psalm 46:10: Be *still*! We find listening very difficult when we maintain a frenetic lifestyle and feel so distracted.
- Proverbs 1:32-33: We find the way to security in listening prayer.
- Philippians 4:4-7: Rejoice anyway: the place of a trust attitude in prayer.
- Philippians 4:8-9: Think on these things: the positive focus of trusting prayer.
- Matthew 7:7-8: Keep on praying: the perseverance of prayer.
- Romans 8:26-27: The Spirit helps us to pray, especially when we feel too weak to pray.

- Matthew 26:39: Yielding prayer follows Jesus' model in Gethsemane. What do you need to yield to cooperate with God?
- 2 Corinthians 12:7-10: Sometimes God does not grant our requests, but always gives us the better gift—the one that accomplishes His benevolent will.
- Matthew 9:37-38: Jesus encourages selfless prayers—for God's will to be done in others' lives.
- 1 Thessalonians 5:17: It never ceases—think about that!

Prayer Maturing

Prayer cannot be mastered, but our couple and individual praying can mature. Do you see at this chapter's end what that means? Maturing prayer reflects the selfless touch of God's Spirit on the minds and hearts of the prayers, transforming the prayers offered from self-centered to God-centered acts of continual communication.

Don't be hard on yourselves if now your prayers tend to recite to God a list of wants and perceived needs. God cares about what you need and want. Over time, however, the Spirit will lead you to care more about what He desires and is doing around you. You will find yourself seeking to understanding and cooperate more with what God desires than what you want. Your prayers flip—God leads you to be concerned for others first; you lower your wants and needs to second place because you trust that God is taking care of you. That's a certain sign of maturing prayer. Trust the Spirit in you. Keep on praying. The Spirit will keep on transforming you through worship, Bible reading/study, and prayer!

CHAPTER 8:

Cooperating with God – Service

Service often follows maturing, selfless praying. As God invites you as a couple to cooperate with Him in what He's doing in others, you find yourselves pointed toward another. That other may be your spouse. Often God directs the two of you toward someone else. You may know of a neighbor facing surgery and feel prompted to cook a meal. Perhaps the thought of a specific couple recurs over a few days. You realize that God has invited you to contact and encourage them. The response to the prompting amounts to obedience to God as service to another. The response to God's prompting opens the door of the Service Discipline.

Jesus responded to God's prompting to serve others. Since God uses the Spiritual Disciplines to transform our lives into Christlikeness, we may rightly assume that helping others will become central in our life as well. After all, Jesus challenged His twelve closest disciples with these words:

> You know that those who are regarded as rulers of the Gentiles lord it over them, and their high officials exercise authority over them. Not so with you. Instead, whoever wants to become great among you must be your servant, and whoever wants to be first must be slave of all. For even the Son of Man did not come to be served, but to serve, and to give his life as a ransom for many.
>
> Mark 10:42-45 (NIV)

More Than Words

Jesus made God's love real through service. His teaching impressed people and burned in their hearts, but His words alone did not effect God's changes.

We who are parents understand how our actions teach more powerfully than our words. I remember teaching our daughters about forgiveness. A little tiff created a moment of drama between them. I stepped in to teach them how to ask for and grant forgiveness. My sage teaching extracted a halfhearted "I'm sorry. Forgive me?"

This was followed by an equally weak "I forgive you."

Yet both girls were watching a few days later when I said something that hurt Mary Beth. They closely watched as I swallowed my pride, admitted my wrongdoing, and asked for forgiveness. They witnessed Mary Beth disregard her pain and grant me forgiveness. We ended the moment with a long embrace. When we parted, the storm clouds in our kitchen had lifted.

A few days later, our daughters were arguing about a doll. The harsh words gave way to a shove and waterworks. I intervened again. This time, when it came time to reconcile, I could refer to what they'd seen between Mom and me. This time my daughters' apology and forgiveness sounded more heartfelt.

Words will never suffice, and actions give flesh to belief. Service incarnates the teaching of Jesus.

Actions for Others

Service pictures one person prompted and enabled by God, humbly moving toward another person to accomplish God's best. Marriage best captures God's intention when each spouse follows Jesus into self-denying sacrificial service toward the other. Selfless service becomes a useful tool that allows God's best will to be accomplished in their mate.

As you practice the Spiritual Discipline of service, know that your spouse deserves your selfless sacrifice most of all. You may be tempted to look beyond the home first, but don't. Let the relationship under your roof receive your best and most frequent service.

I learned this the hard way, or better put, Mary Beth suffered most when I learned this the hard way. As a pastor, I often failed to realize that my wife and children deserved my best service. For the first ten years of my pastoral career, our family had only two full weeks of vacation out of twenty. I was called back to conduct a funeral every other time.

The last straw occurred when I was called back for the third time in one week. To make matters worse, we were vacationing five hours from our South Georgia home.

Over that decade, my family lost weeks of fun and relaxation; they lost my attention. Our relationships suffered because I misunderstood the importance of giving my family one week of uninterrupted time. I served the church family while I ignored my family.

This extraordinary week taught me a valuable lesson about serving my family. If I were going to remain available 24/7 to the congregations I served, my family deserved at least two weeks each year when I would be available 24/7.

Expect for God to present opportunities to serve others, far and wide. As a couple, you will help others, but realize that the most important "other" God calls you to serve stands by you in life.

From Occasional Acts to a Lifestyle

Early in the believer's life, service is perceived as an isolated act. The discipline you share may begin this way: You cook that meal for the sick neighbor. You cut the grass of the neighbor who just lost a parent. You keep friends' kids so they may go to a wedding. All these instances provide selfless, sacrificial service.

Don't be surprised, however, if other opportunities present. You may be asked to serve in the congregation's children's ministry. You may be drawn to some other regular service, like greeting guests on Sunday morning or delivering meals to homebound members. Now your service multiplies into a series of servant acts.

God's not finished with you yet. Before you transition to the next life, the Spirit will groom you for a servant lifestyle. Your desire to serve as Christ's emissary matures into a constant readiness to deny self and take up Christ's cross on behalf of another.

Its Own Reward

I've watched repeatedly as individuals and couples advanced in this discipline faster than in others. Why? I think some couples see quick and profound results as they selflessly serve someone.

You see, service contains its own reward. You may need to spend months seeing significant results in Bible study. Many spend years developing a sound prayer life. However, when couples serve and witness the impact made on a person or family, they become hooked on serving.

Some months ago, several men from the church I pastored gathered their wood-splitting gear and we met at the home of a couple we did not know. The elderly husband and wife suffered from major physical issues. They heated half of their home primarily with a wood stove, but neither could split wood. They could carry a few pieces to the stove but lacked the strength to split it. The physical limitations hurt the husband, who was a Vietnam veteran. He had been strong and independent most of his life.

Six other men and I spent four hours splitting logs in the veteran's yard and stacked them near the house. The grateful man called a couple of us into his home to thank us twice, as did the couple's daughter. The daughter's friend thanked us, and a granddaughter thanked all of us profusely with tears. On that day, the blessers received the greatest blessing. So goes the reward of service.

The gratitude reward warms the heart, but Christlike service sacrifices no less even when no gratitude follows. Jesus counseled that we not allow the left hand to know what the right hand does (Matt. 6:3, NIV). We may well serve in secret because the greatest reward tallies in the heart. God places His smile on the heart of the faithful, humble servant.

When you serve as a couple, you know a deep satisfaction from being divinely used. God poured His life-transforming, life-enriching power through you and into another. The tandem-hulled catamaran carries more passengers than a mono-hulled vessel!

God's Smile on Your Hearts

The results need not be evident because God puts His smile on your heart.

Know that God plans for us as individuals and as a couple to be His ears to hear others' weary voices, His arms to support the weak, His hands to sew a hem or split a log. God will use our halting voices to speak His encouragement. God will use our imperfect lives to reflect His love.

God intends to invite you to cooperate with Him in what He's doing in others' lives. He rejoices to share with you the blessings He brings to His children. He shares with us His joy and often their gratitude.

The worshiping couple engaged in transformational Bible reading/study and maturing prayer will develop servants' hearts.

♱ SERVICE DEVOTIONAL STARTERS

Don't forget to do the following with each of the passages you choose:

- Passage: Read the verses over a couple of times.
- Past: What did the author say to the original hearers/readers?
- Present: What caught my attention in the passage? Share with your spouse.
- Prayer: Turn the thoughts impressed on you by God's abiding Spirit into a prayer.

Keep a record of your daily devotionals; note the passage, the original message, the message to you, and the prayer arising from the present application.

- John 13:3-8: Washing begets washing for Jesus' followers.
- John 13:16-17: Service conveys the humility of our Master.
- Acts 3:1-10: Christlike service requires humility and may be seen as scandalous.
- Romans 12:14-16: Paul identifies several examples of service.
- John 19:16-18: Jesus' ultimate act of service on the cross informs all our Christlike service.

- Colossians 1:10-12: Service is essential to the "worthy life."
- Colossians 3:23-24: Though addressed to household slaves, this advice applies to us as God's servants.
- Ephesians 2:8-10: We were redeemed to be God's tools of others' redemption.
- Acts 20:35: Selfless giving (service) garners more blessings than selfish receiving (greed).
- 1 Thessalonians 4:11-12: This verse emphasizes the value of quiet service.

God desires for us as spouses to mirror Jesus' servant attitude. As the Spirit guides us into more Christlikeness, we can expect to experience a growing desire to serve our spouse.

CHAPTER 9:

From a Taking to a Giving Life – Generosity

G enerosity as a spiritual attitude means that any person or couple practicing it finds themselves aligned with a primary perspective of the Creator. From the first chapter of the Bible to the last, we read of a giving Creator, Redeemer, and Sustainer. As Creator, in Genesis 1, Father God fashioned the universe then gave the caretaking over to the human beings He created. As Redeemer, God the Son gave Himself to suffer the consequences of our self-centeredness. As Sustainer, God the Spirit provides purpose, provision, and protection to all who accept His invitation into the eternal relationship by faith. The disciplines of worship,

Bible reading/study, and prayer focus on a God who gives. Worship refocuses our vision. Reading and studying Scripture grabs hold of our minds with a transforming revelation of who God is. Then maturing prayer leads us to hear God's desires over the howling inner voice of *want* that our media cultivate daily.

Contrast God's generous nature with the spirit of our time. We live in an age of conspicuous consumption, another expression of self-centeredness.

As a pastor preparing couples for marriage and performing weddings, I witnessed many couples drive themselves into deep wedding debt before marriage. They heaped the debt for a memorable wedding on top of college loan debt, loans for new automobiles, and perhaps a mortgage. According to Businessinsider.com,[5] recent research puts marriage costs in the US—from ring to honeymoon—at an average of $38,700.

We live in a materialistic and greedy culture. Yet what else do we expect from our culture? We grow up in a self-centered society the way a fish grows up in an aquarium. The constraints of the glass appear natural to the fish born there. The fish does not see the glass walls as restricting or limiting. But it has never swum in the sea.

---

5   "A staggering percentage of couples are going into debt to pay for their weddings — here are the countries where the problem is the worst," by Erin McDowell, BusinessInsider.com, https://www.businessinsider.com/wedding-cost-go-into-debt-pay-couples-2019-7

Likewise, materialism seems natural to us. In our culture, we equate success with the acquisition of possessions. We enter adulthood with the notion that owning more things brings greater happiness. When we possess an extra dollar, we've been programmed to think of how we may spend that dollar on ourselves. Thinking about another's need rarely crosses our radar; we simply think of ourselves.

Generosity, therefore, stands as one of the most critical Spiritual Disciplines for Western Christians. Why? Dallas Willard, Baptist clergyman and philosophy professor, wrote: "The spiritually wise person has always known that frivolous consumption corrupts the soul away from trust in, worship of, and service to God and injures our neighbors as well."[6]

Richard Foster, Willard's friend and church historian, stated a similar sentiment in positive terms: "Simplicity sets us free to receive the provision of God as a gift that is not ours to keep and can be freely shared with others."[7]

Few of us stand in a position to significantly influence society. Still, every believing couple may color our corner of society with a lifestyle of generosity that flows from simplicity, or frugality.

---

6   Dallas Willard, *The Spirit of the Disciplines: Understanding How God Changes Lives* (San Francisco: HarperOne, 1988), 169.

7   Richard Foster, *Celebration of Disciplines, 20th Anniversary Edition* (San Francisco: HarperSanFrancisco, 1998), 85.

In contrast to our consumptive culture, we remember some of Jesus' most oft-quoted words, preserved by John's quill (John 3:16, NIV): "God so loved the world that he gave his one and only son...." Because God loves, God gives. When God gave His son, He gave extravagantly. God's generosity issues from a selfless sacrifice.

Here we see the basis of a maturing believer's attitude toward possessions, whether material, emotional, or spiritual.

Like Father, Like Children

God created us in His image. God showed a generous nature by sharing creation with us. Further, God allowed His son to pay a debt of right living we could not pay. Accepting these premises, we understand that our heavenly Father desires us to reflect His generosity. The spiritual discipline of simplicity, or frugality, leads the believer or the maturing couple to a generous lifestyle.

Simplicity never sees possessions as evil; neither does this spiritual discipline extol poverty as some virtue. The couple practicing simplicity may expect to see all possessions as expressions of God's generosity. What if we receive all possessions as gifts and receive them gratefully? The blessings from God enrich our lives but then become blessings from God through us to others.

Our Spiritual DNA

Paul wrote to the Galatian believers about the "fruit of the Spirit." This odd-to-us language describes the formation of God's character in our character. God's Spirit brings God's characteristics to bear on our nature. Think of it as the Spirit seeding the garden of our soul with God's life. As we cultivate the Spirit's life, that seed grows into a transformed human character. Consequently, we bear the fruit of "love, joy, peace, patience, kindness, goodness, faithfulness, gentleness, and self-control" (Gal. 5:22 and 23a, NIV).

Each of the fruits of the Spirit exists more for others than for us. Think about the fruit trees you've seen. Did the apple tree keep the apples for itself? Did the pear tree stingily hold onto its fruit, refusing to release it? What would the plum tree or fig tree gain by hoarding its fruit?

Instead, trees drop fruit on the ground for animals to be nourished, people to enjoy, and the soil to reabsorb for nutrients. Likewise, the spiritual fruit God cultivates in us exists primarily for others. The different spiritual fruit born in our marriages serves to nourish many around us. We can produce the fruit of God's character because the Spirit grafts God's nature to our character-tree.

Our Generosity Challenge

Generosity may be one of the most difficult spiritual seeds to bear fruit because we live in a materialism-soaked society. Madison Avenue constantly bombards our minds with inducements to spend every penny. At every turn, we're told that life will not be acceptable unless we purchase a particular product.

The American Psychological Association reckons that children see forty thousand advertisements per year. These powerful messages fashioned by highly trained adults are aimed at the minds of children who cannot yet decide the suitability of the content.[8] Believing couples must fight the conditioning of hundreds and thousands of potent messages to be transformed into frugal and generous teams.

Easier Together

Thankfully, a couple has two advantages. First, they both have God's Spirit exerting divine influence on their willing hearts. We need God's power on our side to counteract the years of conditioning exerted on us by TVs, smartphones, and tablets.

Second, couples better meet this idolatrous challenge together. God intends for you to deny yourself (take the

---

8   Wilcox, B. L., Ph.D., Kunkel, D., Ph.D., Cantor, J., Ph.D., Dowrick, P., Ph.D., Linn, S., Ph.D., & Palmer, E., Ph.D.2004. (2004, February 20). The APA Task Force on Advertising and Children. Retrieved January 20, 2021, from https://www.apa.org/pubs/info/reports/advertising-children#:~:text=It%20is%20estimated%20that%20advertisers,over%20those%20from%20the%201970s.

focus off yourself) and take up the cross daily for your honey (i.e., seek what God is doing in your spouse today).

I'm not a psychic, but I feel confident that God will use you often to help your beloved deal with the temptations of materialism. Each of us possesses a level of spiritual immunity to the Mammon virus (Matt. 6:19-21 and 24). According to Matthew's Gospel, Jesus warned us of the shortsighted nature of storing up treasures in this life. He went on to say that we will either serve God or Mammon (the personification of greed). Our imperfect human nature seeks security in what we can see and hold and count. We easily fall prey to Mammon's wiles. We may find ourselves worshiping at the altar of materialism before we realize it. Every day our natural tendencies suffer bombardment by frequent messages to complete our happiness through owning or buying a product. We have internal and external temptations!

You've felt and seen how the stresses of life and the reassertion of old human patterns of materialism may tempt you. But take heart: your devotional life together may walk you and your spouse down from materialism's ledge.

Consider this. Your husband dreamed about a set of new golf clubs for months. This month he received a bonus, and he's hot-to-trot to go to the golfing store. You know the money would be better spent finishing off the loan for your son's braces. After praying for the grace to deal kindly with this obvious-to-you Mammon virus infection, you say to him, "Honey, weren't we blessed to have that bonus come in? What should we do?"

When your husband mentions the golf clubs, you say, "Wouldn't that be nice! However, I wonder if we can discuss it. We've talked about getting out from under the high-interest loan for Rich Jr.'s braces. This would pay that off and leave us with a couple hundred dollars. What if we established a savings account for those golf clubs you want, pay off the braces loan, and deposit the balance? We can then channel into your golf club account the hundred dollars we've been paying on the braces each month. We will be out from under that ridiculous interest rate, and in eight or nine months you'll have your new clubs. How does that sound?"

We boys and our expensive toys sometimes let our "wanter" overtake our "thinker." You see where this is going. All of us have those moments of weakness. The question is not if but when we will face the Mammon virus. As a faithful couple, we can encourage and strengthen each other.

Reframing Material Perspective

The transition from a greedy to a generous life happens as we shift our perspective on possessions. Generosity rests on the belief that all a couple possesses comes as a generous gift from God. From childhood, we've been convinced that natural ownership and self-direction lead to the best life. We think, "This is my life, this is my marriage, and this is my car. These are my golf clubs. This is my house. If you don't believe it, look on the mortgage. Okay, the bank owns most of it, but my name is there too!"

Never has that perspective been labeled truthfully. We're talking about a self-centered viewpoint. Notice the number of personal pronouns modifying the possessions listed. I'm reminded of the seagulls in *Finding Nemo*. Every time they entered the story, they all spoke the same line, "Mine! Mine! Mine!"

By God's gracious transforming work, our perspective on this life may shift from "mine" to "gift." The Spirit inspires the human heart to receive all of life as a provision from God.

"But wait, Bill," you interrupt. "I worked for that bonus. I pay for that mortgage and the car loans and those terribly expensive braces. How can you say these are gifts?"

Point well taken, except that generosity helps us see that the strength and health to work daily come from God. Generosity acknowledges God's benevolent hand in opening the door for a good job. God's love for you manifests as circumstances that led you and your honey together and now help keep you together.

Our efforts do not negate God as the source of our generous provision. Look at it this way. For years you've wanted a shiny new Corvette. Amazingly, your father says, "Son, I want to give you a portion of your inheritance so I can watch you enjoy it. Here are the keys to my new Corvette. I bought it for you, and it's yours when I die. All I ask is that you take me for a drive now and then so I can see your joy."

Would you keep the car clean and polished? Would you take your dad for a weekly drive if he were able? Of course you would, and you would enjoy washing and waxing that vehicle. You could let someone else detail it, except that you prefer to do it yourself. You clean her up every time you return from a drive.

Now, does your effort to clean and maintain the Corvette negate the gift from dad? No, and neither does my endeavor to write this book negate that God enables me to write, the calling to write, and the opportunity to finish the book.

Our perspective on life and things must be reframed from possessiveness to generosity for us to cooperate with God in His life and work here on earth.

Open Hand versus Closed Fist

That generous perspective leads to a charitable lifestyle. I like to picture the difference between the philanthropic heart and the greedy heart as the difference between an open hand and a closed fist.

I'm reminded of Paul's use of a similar picture in the letter to the Philippians. In describing the life toward which we believers aspire, Paul challenged the ancient Greek believers with these words: "In other words, adopt the mindset of Jesus the Anointed. Live with His attitude in your hearts. Remember: Though He was in the form of God, He chose *not to cling to* equality with God…" (Phil. 2:5- 6, The Voice, emphasis added).

The eternal Christ opened His hand, as it were, to release possession of equality with the Father. He opened His hand so that He could cooperate with the Father's will to redeem us. The Father opened His hand to release the Son to take on the creature's life. Jesus lived it in a relationship with God exactly as the Father intended we live with Him from the inception. He completed God's eternal plan by dying in our place to pay the full consequences for our broken relationship with the Father.

The eternal Son opened His hand to take on human life with all its challenges, pain, and temptations. He then lived and died to fulfill the Father's love for us. In the Father's and Son's acts of "opening their hands," we see divine generosity.

The Spirit now works in us to recreate the image of God's generosity. By this discipline, God intends to lead us to the open-handed love toward others as He has been open-handedly loving toward us.

Start!

How do we cooperate with God in this transformation? As a couple, you respond with some planned, proportional giving to your congregation and other charities.

As you go through the passages below, open your mind to extending your hand. Take the first small step toward generosity. If this attitude feels too new and uncomfortable, remember that your Father smiles when you respond to His prompting in the smallest of ways. Even as we human parents smile when a baby responds to our prompting to take those first, tottering steps, so God finds pleasure in our halting efforts.

The greatest challenge comes in releasing what you've counted as security so that you can reach forward for those first steps. Your most primitive brain will see this as a threat and throw up all kinds of warning signals. You will find many reasons not to give until you develop the habit of giving.

However, give anyway. All you have is God's gift. God encourages you to cooperate with Him in being open-handed. You may only be generous if you release your grip. You give, and God will bless you and the one who receives because you became a symbol of His loving generosity.

Grow!

As a faithful and obedient couple, your intentional responses, like study, planned giving, and deaccumulation, act like fertilizer to your soul. I believe that every couple who responds to God's prompting to give will find that giving feels good. God likes to share. As you two give, God smiles in your hearts. You want that smile to remain, so you sense the nudge to give again, followed by another heart-smile.

Eventually, you realize other, more significant ways to cooperate with God. That may mean moving toward tithing your income. You don't want to tithe to check a box, but you move toward tithing as the next step in your growing attitude of generosity.

Maybe you decide to rewrite your will to leave part of your estate to a ministry or charity. My wife and I presently have wills that direct a percentage of our estate to our alma maters when the last one transitions to heaven.

You may wish to double-up on the attitude of generosity by reducing what you own that you do not need, but others could use. Look in your closet. What have you not worn in the past season? Do you have six coats but only use two or three? Why not take the other three or four to the local clothes closet? What about shoes? Could others use those pumps you haven't worn in a couple of years? The goodwill for Goodwill may continue to touch every aspect of your life—kitchen, workshop, library, you name it!

De-accumulating helps others as you lighten the load of items you rarely or no longer use.

Traveling Lighter

Catamaran spirituality makes you a sleek, seaworthy vessel. Generosity lightens the spiritual vessel's unnecessary ballast, so she travels lighter. Traveling lighter and a nimbler response to God are two unexpected benefits of generosity. May your generosity discipline lighten your load and make you faster to respond to God's promptings.

GENEROSITY DEVOTIONAL STARTERS

As you continue reading and discussing the passages below, why not make a list of first steps that enter your thinking and discussions. Allow the Spirit to plant suggestions in your mind that lead to a fruitful couple discussion and to decisions. Don't forget to do the following with each of the passages you choose:

- Passage: Read the verses over a couple of times.
- Past: What did the author say to the original hearers/readers?
- Present: What caught my attention in the passage? Share with your spouse.
- Prayer: Turn the thoughts God impresses on you by His abiding Spirit into a prayer.

Keep a record of your daily devotionals; note the passage, the original message, the message to you, and the prayer arising from the present application.

- Acts 2:44-45: Notice the changes in families and the whole congregation!
- Proverbs 11:25: Generosity blesses the receiver and the giver in God's economy of life.
- Mark 12:41-44: The widow teaches us about the radical trust beneath generosity.
- Matthew 25:34-40: When generous to another, you give twice: once to the person and once to the Lord, but both at the same time.
- 2 Corinthians 9:6-8: Cheerful giving best captures God's generosity and avails the giver of God's abundant provision for further giving.
- 2 Corinthians 8:3-5: The Macedonian believers (Philippians) gave first to the Lord and then to Paul. They gave beyond their means because the generous attitude they had developed informed them that God always gave them enough and more.
- Proverbs 19:17: This compares favorably with Matthew 25:40, where God receives any act of generosity or kindness toward another as if given to Him.

- Luke 6:38: Though this word fits in Jesus' warning against judgment, it still serves as a warning against greedy living. It points us to the spiritual consequences God works into our world that govern all relationships.

- Malachi 3:10: Is this trying to manipulate the Lord by giving the tithe? No, I think this is the consequence set by God as a law of relationships. We avail ourselves of this law by our giving or withholding.

- Luke 19:1-10: What changes in attitude toward possessions have been wrought in your life since "meeting Jesus?"

Learning to Live Open-handedly

The very nature of God may be represented by the open hand. Even Paul acknowledged divine open-handedness when he wrote to the Philippian believers:

> Your attitude should be the same as that of Christ Jesus: 6 who, though he was in the form of God, did not count equality with God a thing to be grasped (i.e., to be held on to), 7 but emptied himself (i.e., opened his grip on equality to serve), by taking the form of a servant, being born in the likeness of men.
>
> Philippians 2:5-7, ESV (comments mine)

When we grow in grace through the Spiritual Disciplines, we realize how God frequently opens His hand to release blessing into and through us. The transforming, supra-natural response moves us to open our hands too.

CHAPTER 10:

Wowed by God! – Gratitude

We take a step now onto the last steppingstone discipline: gratitude. In a way, this discipline brings us full circle back to the first discipline, worship. Gratitude may constitute the purest form of worship. Meister Eckhart, a thirteenth-century German theologian, philosopher, and mystic, wrote, "If the only prayer you ever say in your entire life is thank you, it will be enough." In this one statement, Eckhart combines worship, prayer, and gratitude.

I included this comment to demonstrate the interrelated nature of the disciplines. By now you have realized this interrelationship and have blended disciplines. Each one enriches the others, and gratitude amplifies the others best of all.

Gratitude Is...

Gratitude describes a thankful or appreciative feeling that arises after we recognize a kind act or some word that elicits a positive emotion. Gratitude changes one's life, even if only for a moment.

The feelings of gratitude usually ebb and flow with our circumstances. That favor done for us warms our hearts with thankfulness. We express gratitude in the form of words of thanks or a thank-you note. After the event or effort, our gratitude fades with the memory. When something prods our memory of kindness, we may again feel gratitude—ebb and flow.

In a relationship with God, we find a different rhythm of gratitude. As we practice the Spiritual Disciplines over time, we find our awareness of God's benevolent presence. We realize that God abides with us always. The name "Immanuel" given to Joseph for Jesus by the angel proves to be our experience: "God with us" (Matt. 1:20-23).

Recognizing our heavenly Father's continual presence in the Spirit also prompts awareness of the gift of Himself. God provides the spiritual gifts of an undeserved relationship by giving Himself to us daily. Our Father provides the material provision needed and the strength and opportunity to acquire and enjoy it. He sets before us promises for our future, both here and hereafter.

Gratitude flows with the never-ending gifts of and from God. What does this mean? We experience gratitude as a relentless stream of emotion following God's lavishly flowing gifts. Spiritually speaking, the couple who practices the discipline of appreciation will come to the place of ever-flowing, never-ebbing thankfulness.

Growing a Grateful Disposition

Maturing gratitude looks more like a lifestyle than an isolated incident. Ah, here's the purpose of the gratitude discipline—developing a grateful disposition. We're practicing toward the goal of a grateful temperament. In my first book, *Marriage Maximized: The Guide to a Purposeful and Passionate Relationship*, I discussed the negative brain bias (NBB). Briefly, NBB describes the tendency most humans develop to see the negatives around them first. Neuroscientists report that our innate fight-or-flight response to perceived danger accounts for this bias. Our practice of the fight-or-flight response develops neural pathways over time that allow frequent fearful, negative reactions. Our brains become wired to and biased toward the negative responses.

Well, gratitude rewires the brain for a positive brain bias. We will continue to respond to perceived threats instantly with our natural fight-or-flight response. Over time and with practice, however, we can develop a will to look first and be thankful for the good when the threat does not exist.

What would happen to your marriage if gratitude changed from an occasional feeling into a disposition, a state of being continually grateful?

The Grateful Couple

A pervasive gratitude attitude spreads over all of life like a blanket of light, enabling the couple to see good things in all circumstances because God abides in them. Gratitude may not remove the burdens of life, but it lightens the load we carry. Gratitude lifts our sight heavenward. It disposes us to hope, expecting God's comforting and transforming presence in all our difficulties. Just as it reduces our burden, thankfulness multiplies our joys.

Picture for a moment the benefits of a grateful disposition in your marriage. What if your burdens were lightened and your joys doubled? Here's a practical example. Assume you carelessly run your car into a ditch and call a wrecker to extract it. Your vehicle is drivable, but the repairs will cost hundreds of dollars and your car insurance will probably increase. In the face of all this, you dread telling your spouse that evening, but gratitude colors your marriage.

When you tell your spouse, fearful of the response, your husband's grateful disposition rises in his face and words: "Oh, honey, I'm so thankful that you're okay!" He hugs you close then says, "God spared you, and I believe He will guide us through this. Now, what did the insurance company say?"

Brain-Changing Gratitude

A thankful bearing can emerge from a rewired brain. The more we exercise gratitude, the more grateful we become, and science now confirms this. The more often we choose gratitude for the silver lining over criticism about the dark clouds, the more we rewire our negative brain bias to a positive brain bias.

Robert Emmons teaches positive psychology and researches its effects at the University of California at Davis. In 2007, he wrote the book *Thanks! How Practicing Gratitude Can Make You Happier*. Read some of the significant findings from his gratitude study:

> Our groundbreaking research has shown that grateful people experience higher levels of positive emotions such as joy, enthusiasm, love, happiness, and optimism, and that the practice of gratitude as a discipline protects a person from the destructive impulses of envy, resentment, greed, and bitterness. We have

discovered that a person who experiences gratitude is able to cope more effectively with everyday stress, may show increased resilience in the face of trauma-induced stress, and may recover more quickly from illness and benefit from greater physical health. Our research has led us to conclude that experiencing gratitude leads to increased feelings of connectedness, improved relationships, and even altruism. We have also found that when people experience gratitude, they feel more loving, more forgiving, and closer to God. Gratitude, we have found, maximizes the enjoyment of the good – our enjoyment of others, of God, of our lives.[9]

Emmons outlines some of the brain-changed results the grateful couple may expect. His attractive list makes the discipline of gratitude attractive, huh?

Recipe for a Discipline

Choosing to act in a particular manner consistently over a long period defines a discipline. Gratitude may be developed if we discipline ourselves with a simple process: stop-look-act. Stop moving long enough to see what's around you. Look at the people around you. Did you

9   Robert Emmons, *Thanks!* (Boston: Houghton Mifflin, 2007), 10-11.

notice the restaurant server doing an exceptional job, or did you hear that genuine "thank you" from the person you held the door for?

Now that you've slowed your pace, look at your circumstances. Is the sun shining? Do you feel well? Is traffic traveling safer today? Where do you see God's fingerprints on the activities of today? Do you see it?

Finally, act by expressing your thanks to God. Maybe you sing a song of thanks while driving in the better-than-usual traffic. Do you write a thank-you note to the colleague who gave you that word of encouragement before an important presentation? You may never again see the young man behind the Chick-fil-A counter who seemed genuinely pleased to serve, so you choose to pass his positive attitude along to someone you meet.

Charles M. Shelton, a Catholic priest and psychologist, made an impact on Robert Emmons' life. In 2010, Shelton wrote *The Gratitude Factor: Enhancing Your Life through Grateful Living*. He recommended a four-part "Daily Gratitude Inventory: Pause, Review, Relish, and Respond."[10] At day's end, pause. The two of you may take a few minutes at dinner or just before bed to put a comma in the day before applying the period. In those moments, review the day, looking for the good. The bad will be easier to see, but we're training our minds to recognize the good things and the God-things.

10   Charles M. Shelton, *The Gratitude Factor: Enhancing Your Life through Grateful Living* (Muhwah, NJ: Hidden Springs, 2010), 22-26.

Once you have identified several blessings, relish together the positives. Describe them in detail. Remember them. Draw back into your consciousness the good thoughts and feelings surrounding the memory. Share those thoughts and feelings together. The more you can share these good things, the more likely you will look for tomorrow's positives and go through this exercise again. Finally, respond. Turn your relishing into thanksgiving to God. Acknowledge God as the giver of all good gifts, as James wrote in James 1:17. The process may take only five or ten minutes, but the benefits are abundant. This short inventory will help your brain build a positive bias, strengthen the relationship between you, improve your relationship with God, and prepare you for a better day tomorrow. That's worth a few minutes!

Shelton's four parts of this exercise may serve well to help you build a more intentionally grateful life. If you can devise an intentional process that better fits you as a couple, great! Sharing gratitude for the good in your marriage and in your individual lives remains the goal. As the Nike ads said for years, *Just Do It*.

So will you and your partner take a few minutes daily to put on your gratitude? Emmons and Shelton give suggestions, but you two can be creative with your own gratitude discipline. Make it fun and do it regularly. Don't beat yourself up when you miss a day of showing gratitude. Just start again. It's not how many times you fail but how many times you start over that makes for a gratefully disciplined life.

Notice the Benefits of a Grateful Marriage

The seeds of discipline planted by the Spirit in your marriage, when frequently nourished, will yield their sweet fruit. Here's a list of gratitude's benefits, although you will discover many more:

- sweeter marriage environment
- kinder, gentler home relationships
- modeling Christlikeness to the kids
- deeper satisfaction in life with a positive outlook and expectation
- brightening your corner of the world with a positive outlook
- encouraging others to respond to your gratitude with gratitude, creating a gratitude ripple effect

Gratitude Attitude

God uses the discipline of gratitude to pull a marriage from the rat-race rut and set it on the gratefully purposeful marriage path. Gratitude serves as one of the most robust supports to bind spouses' faith into catamaran spirituality.

Look for the good each day. Seek the best in people. Mark the grace notes in your circumstances. Expect God to bless you, then praise Him for it all. It is better to live each day enraptured by God's presence and provision than to live each day aggravated and frustrated by the myriad little annoyances along the way.

Today looks like a great day to don your gratitude attitude.

GRATITUDE DEVOTIONAL STARTERS

The passages below remind you of many reasons for gratitude. Allow them to set the tone for your day; use them as your starting blocks for the race. Here are suggestions for how to read and discuss each of the passages you choose:

- Passage: Read the verses over a couple of times.
- Past: What did the author say to the original hearers/readers?
- Present: What caught my attention in the passage? Share with your spouse.
- Prayer: Turn the thoughts God impresses on you by His Spirit into a prayer.

May I suggest that you take a few minutes each evening to survey the day. I like Shelton's four-part Daily Gratitude

Inventory. I would only change "pause" to "rest" or "relax" to keep the "R" alliteration going.

- Psalm 100:4-5: Can you picture yourselves entering God's throne room hand-in-hand? Try to imagine the gratitude that may well up in you in the presence of God.

- James 1:17: James encouraged his readers to acknowledge God as the source of all good gifts.

- Psalm 40:1-3: Think back on the last time God extracted you from some "slimy pit." What did you feel? How did you express gratitude? Gratitude is never offered too late or too often.

- Psalm 16:5-11: Ask yourself, How can I not express gratitude to the one who gave me this wonderful life?

- Ephesians 1:3: When did you last thank God for your spiritual blessings?

- Lamentations 3:22-23: This most grateful passage falls in the middle of Jeremiah's lament. He teaches us that we may find a reason to thank God in any situation.

- Ephesians 5:19-20: We may offer God thanksgiving at any time, in any circumstances, and with anybody who wishes to join. It's always appropriate.

- Psalm 63:2-5: How would your marriage change if you both believed God's love is the best part of this life?

- Hebrews 12:28-29: We are heirs of the kingdom! Be thankful.

- 1 Thessalonians 5:18: God wills that we live in thankfulness together in all circumstances. Why? Because He never leaves us alone in those tough times.

The Sweet Oxygen of Gratitude in Marriage

A grateful heart connects deeply with others because people respond to the positive nature of a thankful person. In your marriage, gratitude will help fill your relationship with the crisp, clean atmosphere of appreciation. Gratitude slowly replaces the toxic air of anger, frustration, criticism, judgment, and selfishness. A grateful soul lives less and less in these negative attitudes.

Your primary relationships with God and your spouse both benefit and deepen with your growing gratitude.

CHAPTER 11:

Overcoming Inertia

As you deduced from the previous ten chapters, I'm an optimist. I live with high hopes for your progress as a couple in the spiritual life. My optimism rests on my faith and my experience. It's not unrealistic; however, it's time for this optimist to be realistic with you.

The transformation God has in store for you will not be easy. The spiritual life is simple, but it's far from easy. Indeed, it's impossible without the Holy Spirit enabling you to overcome the inertia of your present state. Let's name the issue: we seek a changeless comfort zone. We believe deeply that the good life does not change. If it's pleasing, then it should not change, right?

Yet a survey of life proves that idea false. For instance, God never intended for you and me to remain infants. We were born to grow into adulthood, with lots of changes there.

Then came the day we first stepped into a classroom to begin a long process of intellectual change. Let's see—we had primary school, secondary school, maybe technical college or academic college, and now many of us have graduate degrees. Preschool through a graduate degree may equal more than eighteen years of the challenge to change. God gave us this brain to develop.

Let's not forget the informal emotional education we receive. The trial-and-error of learning how to develop emotional intelligence requires significant changes. God intends for us to move from self-centric emotions to the selflessness of empathy and Christlike compassion.

That brings us to the spiritual life. Well, without change, we miss out on the closeness to God that absolutely and eternally changes us. Some start further away than others because of upbringing. No matter what, God plans to change each of us so we may better experience His love, selflessly love each other, and be used effectively in His kingdom.

In truth we were born to change in every aspect of life.

Ready for Challenges Ahead?

Because we prefer not to leave our individual comfort zone's familiarity, we face several challenges as we embrace the couple's devotional life. Couples following a spiritual discipline find the practice especially challenging. Here are some of the obstacles you will likely encounter.

Time

Every couple will face an inevitable scheduling challenge to make time for a devotional life. I suspect you have already crammed your calendar with activities. You have a work schedule eating up hours of each weekday. In fact, it may eat up whole days if you must travel with your job. You block out time for the gym or to run. If you have children, they may be old enough to be in school, and you may be tasked with taking them to and from school. Maybe your children play some sport after school or have dance, gymnastics, or karate. Of course, we fit worship into that schedule and perhaps a Bible study or monthly committee meeting. What about dentist appointments, grocery shopping, or car maintenance? So where do you wedge into your schedule another ten to twenty minutes daily?

Have you ever considered a values audit? Each of us holds a set of aspirational values, and we live by a set of practical values. That values audit requires spending time as a couple prayerfully asking, "What values do we consider important for building the life God calls us to build?" Your deliberations may take two or three discussions interspersed with prayer. Once your prayer and conversation produce a list of several prioritized values, you then turn to your daily life to identify the values you practice.

To come to that list, you need at least two tools: your calendar and your checkbook register or online banking statement. Take the past six to twelve months of activity and spending—the more extended period covers all the major holidays and anniversaries and vacations. Now list the recurring expenditures of time and money. If your bank and credit card(s) offer an annual breakdown of spending, like groceries, gasoline, restaurants, and entertainment, notice the categories where you spend the most money (and time). Make a list of the most frequent and regular expenditures. Assign to them a practical value. Why go and spend in these areas regularly? This process may take longer than the aspirational values list.

Once you've polished each list, compare them. What aspirational values do you see reflected in your practical values list? Does your daily life reflect the life you believe God called you to live? What aspirational values do not appear on your practical values list?

Now come the hard prayer and discussions. What on your practical values list needs to be reduced, even though you value it enough to give it high practical value? Is one of your high aspirational values absent from your lifestyle? If we believe God calls us to live by a particular aspiration, how do we translate this value into practice? How do we modify our time and energy and money expenditures?

The couples I coach have determined to value their relationship with God and each other enough to log ninety-minute sessions with me. They do the work to cooperate with God's transforming work to maximize their marriage. They sacrifice financially for this most meaningful, beneficial value. Two assertions prove true for each couple: one, they didn't have time for coaching; two, they would not have realized the benefit unless they made the tough calendar, energy, and money decisions.

God holds us in His intention. We realize significant progress when we take our relationship with Him and each other off auto-pilot. That's when we act intentionally with the Spirit's inspiration to grow closer to each other and deeper into God's relationship.

Energy

You're tired after looking at your schedule and realizing the energy drain on your life. You ask yourself, "How will I have the energy to do all I do, plus add the devotional time?" The toll of a busy lifestyle already makes you feel like a zombie on Sunday morning. You wonder where to rob some time and energy to do the couple's devotional life. You already rise early and run past dark-thirty.

The values audit will help to identify the energy-draining low-value priorities in your life. Hopefully, you and your beloved will experience an aha moment when you compare the values lists. When you see how much you have been doing and how little return for your time/energy/money, you may be prepared to shift some priorities and activities. Perhaps you will schedule in some resources for R&R. After all, God calls us to a "sabbath rest." Unlike many employers, God does not see us as machines who need only routine maintenance to run without rest!

Get a good night's sleep. Add some fun to your life without feeling guilty. Fun together and rest will regenerate your energy as a couple. With that newfound energy, you can tackle your devotional time together.

Change

Again, something in the brain resists change—even good change. Whatever you attempt as a couple will surface that resistance. You will find many reasons bubbling up in your mind why you just can't do the couple's devotional today. Expect it; it's normal—not fun, but expected.

Keep the "new leather shoe" feeling in mind. All new shoes, like all new habits, feel stiff at first. If the shoe fits, then wearing over time loosens the leather, which conforms to your foot. The once-uncomfortable shoes become your favorites. I have a pair of loafers on their fourth half-sole, and I hate to think about replacing them. May all our new spiritual habits become as comfortable.

Speed

You will face one last challenge—the challenge of God's pace of change. We live in a microwave-speed culture, but God operates at Crock-Pot speed! When we don't see instant spiritual progress, we respond out of our warp-speed conditioning with the thought, "This isn't working! I'll try something else."

Instead, begin the process with the expressed expectation that you have a lifetime to see significant progress. You see, God does not judge our spiritual progress by the distance we travel but by the dependence we develop. Our heavenly Daddy measures progress and the health of our spiritual life by how much more we trust and follow Him and how much more we do that together. The world uses metrics to measure success, like how many times we attend worship and how much money we give to God's causes. God weighs those actions much less than the motivations behind the time and money invested.

Building together a habit of dependence on God happens only over a long period. Look for small steps of progress over long periods of discipline. Here's one unexpected index of spiritual progress I suggest: measure the intensity of desire. How much more do you desire to be close to your partner and to God? As you grow more dependent, expect to mirror that growth in the intensity of desire for closeness to God and your spouse.

Embracing the Change

Yes, we resist change. Yes, the Spiritual Disciplines we've considered all lead to change—slow and gradual.

Yes, we face a lifelong challenge as we practice the Spiritual Disciplines. Every change asked of us will require extraordinary perseverance. That may be uncomfortable, but your stretched spirit enables you to contain more of God's love. Tempered by faith and experience of God's power and faithfulness, realism prepares and perhaps empowers us to embrace the changes.

The benefits of being drawn closer to God through the Spiritual Disciplines outweigh the challenges we face. As the psalmist wrote, "Taste and see that the LORD is good. Oh, the joys of those who take refuge in him!" (Ps. 34:8, NLT).

Feeling close to God compares well with feeling at home. Spiritually, we only come home when we reconnect closely with our heavenly Father, in whose image we were created.

Here's another fact of faith: the longer we practice the Spiritual Disciplines, the more comfortable we feel. Your discomfort will eventually give way to a holy habit that creates a desire for more of God. Now we're talking!

Embrace the disciplines and the initial challenges. Realize that God will work within the parameters of your disciplined actions. Consistency allows God to transform you as a couple more profoundly. The combination of your discipline and God's grace poured into your effort will move you out of your comfort zone's inertia and give you spiritual momentum.

Gaining Maximized Marriage Momentum

The marriage benefits on the disciplined journey of faith include:

- deepened love
- doubled joy
- settled peace
- growing patience
- unending hope
- multiplied fulfillment and satisfaction in marriage and life
- stabilized life
- passion-filled relationships
- purposeful marriage and life

Do these benefits of closeness to God and each other sound appealing? Well, these are not my promises. God plans these, and more, for you. Furthermore, God will grant you the grace to find a time, place, and the energy and patience to engage Him in these disciplines. He knows our weaknesses; He understands our spiritual inertia. He wants closeness with us more than we want it with Him. God needs only our halting, stumbling effort in which to pour His life. He does not expect perfection from us, but He offers to perfect our actions over time. What does that mean? To perfect our spiritual effort means completing the purpose of that effort. As God fills our effort with His love-power, our hearts desire Him more. Our desire for our heavenly Father begins to reflect the depth of His passion for us. This relationship with God becomes the matter of ultimate concern that shapes all of life. Purpose complete; benefits realized.

A realistic view of practicing the Spiritual Disciplines must acknowledge our present state of spiritual inertia. On the other hand, faith-filled realism also confesses belief in a powerfully loving God to work in our weak human responses. Jesus spoke of mustard-seed faith (Mark 4:31 and 32, NIV), meaning the faith's size counts less than the great potential God infuses in the small seed-faith. Similarly, the size of our effort means less than the power God desires to pour into it.

God's got this! Our inertia presents no problem for Him. Trust Him to help you gain maximum spiritual momentum in your marriage.

I hold hope for you to realize an amazing catamaran spirituality! As one last word of encouragement, I offer this list to explain my hope:

1. God intended marriage—your marriage—to reflect His unity, purpose, and joy.
2. God sent His Son to effect a new relationship for all individuals (and couples) who depend on Him.

3. God's Spirit abides in the slums of our hearts to bring our life and marriage up to the level of love, purpose, and passion He intended.

4. God revealed to us humans several steppingstones that we call Spiritual Disciplines to help us realize His love, purpose, and passion.

5. You show evidence of the Spirit's nudging in the direction of God's love, purpose, and passion because you made it this far through the book!

I have no doubt that God is able as we are willing. My marriage proves that to me. Couples I coach demonstrate that regularly.

Hasn't your turn arrived to follow God's leadership in building that sleek catamaran spirituality? I invite you to read on—just one more short chapter.

CHAPTER 12:

Your Journey Awaits

I offer congratulations for hanging on all the way to the end. I'm encouraged for you. Let the brief exercise of reading to the end of this book serve as a metaphor for your couple's devotional life. Get started; take the disciplines step-by-step; don't give up. Before you know it, you'll look back to the start of your devotional time together from farther down the path than you realized!

You're Ready

Go on now. Your couple's devotional journey with its challenges and all its promise awaits you. Remember, you begin with small steps.

Settle on time and place together

At first the discipline of spending ten minutes together may prove more important than the insights gained. Doing facetime with your beloved while traveling speaks loudly of your commitment to God and each other. God will use it!

Be consistent

Don't be discouraged if your consistency suffers for a short time. Get back into the routine. Your spirit needs the routine as much as your body.

Choose one discipline to practice

Give it a couple of weeks minimum before moving on. Take advantage of the resources in the last chapter. They will be helpful, and you will find other resource recommendations within each. I hope these recommended books and websites become part of your provision for the journey.

Basic equipment

In this book, you've collected some of the essential equipment for the voyage set before you. Use these six disciplines to develop your couple's devotional time with God. They will serve you well if you utilize them. Don't see them as ends in themselves. See them as means to the end of a deeper relationship with God and each other. They compare to the hammer, nails, and wood, not the finished structure. They help you build the spiritual house. You focus on the house, not the tools to construct it.

Trust these time-proven disciplines as the tools God will use in your devotional efforts to build a catamaran to carry you on this journey with God. The Son purchased the right to sail with God. The Spirit gives the strength and ability and knowledge to build your two lives into one spiritually. The Father calls you closer so you can journey with Him.

For My Clients

You may be one of the couples who have finished my primary couple's coaching process. This book is for you. You and I have traveled a leg of the journey together. What a privilege you afforded me to share your journey. Thank you for granting me this honor. What a privilege granted by God to be called as your guide for a brief time. Father, I can only pray that You accomplished what You wanted either because of (or despite) my efforts. Thank You for the gift of serving You.

I trust this book will help you gain spiritual momentum as a couple. If you're ready to travel without a guide, blessings on your journey. I trust we will see each other along the Way here and share together the hereafter.

If you want a guide for your voyage, know that I relish the thought and look forward to our journey. I benefit from our time together. Your faithful effort encourages me.

Guide Available

You may have found this book online or in a bookstore. As you look toward your future, you may wish for a bit of help to get started as a couple developing a devotional life. The beginning of a journey holds the most excitement and the most anxiety. You look out over the sea of God's great kingdom and can't wait to embark. You anticipate the refitting of your marriage from two separate boats sailing with God into a twin-hulled spiritual vessel. You understand some of the benefits of catamaran spirituality and can hardly wait until God refits you two into one.

Perhaps you find the maiden voyage of your catamaran spirituality a bit daunting. You two may wish to have a more experienced guide and navigator aboard. I am available!

If God leads in that direction, I'll coach you through the first few miles of developing your couple's spiritual life. Let's talk about whether God is calling us to sail together for a while. On my website, www.selflesslove.net, you will find a *Let's Talk* drop-down menu on the front page's upper right. Choose an available time on my calendar for a Discovery Call.

The Discovery Call amounts to a thirty- to forty-five-minute obligation-free call to discover if God is calling us to work together. I'll listen to your responses to several questions to understand what you need and determine if I can help you. I offer a 10 percent discount to anyone who comes from my book into coaching.

I look forward to hearing from you.

Well, your journey together with God awaits. Whether or not I'm part of that journey as a coach, thank you for allowing me to share with you through my book.

God's blessing on your voyage. Bon voyage!

Want to Dive Deeper?

As you sampled the six Spiritual Disciplines highlighted in my book, you may have felt drawn to explore one or two a bit deeper. Don't ignore that thought—it may well be a holy nudge, like the ones described in chapter 7 on listening prayer.

Below I have listed several resources that I find helpful. May God lead you to find inspiration in them, and may they strengthen your Spiritual Disciplines, deepen your relationship with God, and elevate your relationship.

Blessings, Bill.

Books on the Christian Life

- Lewis, C. S. *Mere Christianity*. New York: Macmillan, 1979.
- Smith, James Bryan. *Embracing the Love of God: The Path and Promise of the Christian Life*. San Francisco: HarperSanFrancisco, 1995.
- Wright, N. T. *Simply Christian: Why Christianity Makes Sense*. San Francisco: HarperSanFrancisco, 2006.

Books on Spiritual Formation and Spiritual Disciplines

- Foster, Richard J. *Celebration of Discipline: The Path to Spiritual Growth, Special 20th Anniversary Edition*. San Francisco: HarperSanFrancisco, 1998.
- Mulholland, M. Robert, Jr. *Invitation to a Journey: A Road Map for Spiritual Formation*. Downers Grove, IL: InterVarsity Press, 1993.
- Willard, Dallas. *The Spirit of the Disciplines: Understanding How God Changes Lives*. New York: HarperOne, 1988.

Books on Bible Study

- Fee, Gordon D. and Douglas Stuart. *How to Read the Bible Book by Book*. Grand Rapids, MI: Zondervan, 2002.

- Foster, Richard J., with Kathryn Helmers. *Life with God: Reading the Bible for Spiritual Transformation.* New York: HarperOne, 2008.
- Mulholland, M. Robert. *Shaped by the Word: The Power of Scripture in Spiritual Formation, Revised Edition.* Nashville, TN: Upper Room Books, 2000.
- Warren, Rick. *Bible Study Methods: Twelve Ways You Can Unlock God's Word.* Grand Rapids, MI: Zondervan, 2006.

Books on Prayer

- Boa, Kenneth. *Face to Face, Vol. 1: Praying the Scriptures for Intimate Worship.* Grand Rapids, MI: Zondervan, 1977.
- Brother Lawrence. *The Practice of the Presence of God with Spiritual Maxims.* Grand Rapids, MI: Spire Books, 20th printing, 2005.
- Foster, Richard J. *Prayer: Finding the Heart's True Home.* New York: HarperCollins, 1992.
- Foster, Richard J. *Sanctuary of the Soul: Journey into Meditative Prayer.* Downers Grove, IL: InterVarsity Press, 2011.
- Guyon, Jeanne. *Experiencing God Through Prayer.* New Kensington, PA: Whitaker House, 1984.
- Hallesby, O. *Prayer.* Translated by Clarence J. Carlsen. Minneapolis, MN: Augsburg Fortress, 1994.

- Laubach, Frank C., PhD. *Prayer: The Mightiest Force in the World*. New York: Fleming H. Revell, 1946. (Available for free download as PDF online. Newer printing also available online.)
- Murray, Andrew. *Living a Prayerful Life*. Minneapolis, MN: Bethany House, 2002.
- Murray, Andrew. *The Believer's School of Prayer*. Minneapolis, MN: Bethany House, 1982.
- Nee, Watchman. *Let Us Pray*. New York: Christian Fellowship Publishers Inc., 1977.
- Underhill, Evelyn. *Abba*. Roger L. Roberts, compiler. A part of Treasures from the Spiritual Classics. Harrisburg, PA: Morehouse Publishing, 1982.
- Yancy, Philip. *Prayer: Does It Make Any Difference?* Grand Rapids, MI: Zondervan, 2006.

Books on Generosity

- Alcorn, Randy. *Managing God's Money: A Biblical Guide*. Carol Stream, IL: Tyndale House, 2011.
- Alcorn, Randy. *Money, Possessions, and Eternity, Revised and Updated Edition*. Wheaton, IL: Tyndale House, 2003.
- Alcorn, Randy. *The Treasure Principle*. Colorado Springs, CO: Multnomah Books, 2001.
- Blanchard, Ken and S. Truett Cathy. *The Generosity Factor: Discover the Joy of Giving Your Time, Talent,*

and Treasure. Grand Rapids, MI: Zondervan, 2002.

- Blue, Ron with Jodie Berndt. *Generous Living: Finding Contentment Through Giving.* Grand Rapids, MI: Zondervan, 1997.

- Foster, Richard J. *Freedom of Simplicity.* San Francisco: HarperSanFrancisco, 1981.

- Foster, Richard J. *Money, Sex, and Power: The Challenge to the Disciplined Life.* San Francisco: Harper & Row, 1985.

- Schnase, Robert. *Practicing Extravagant Generosity: Daily Readings on the Grace of Giving.* Nashville, TN: Abingdon Press, 2011.

- Stanley, Andy. *How to Be Rich: It's Not What You Have. It's What You Do with What You Have.* Grand Rapids, MI: Zondervan, 2013.

Resources on Gratitude

- Emmons, Robert A., PhD. *Thanks! How Practicing Gratitude Can Make You Happier.* New York: Houghton Mifflin, 2007.

- Shelton, Charles M., PhD. *The Gratitude Factor: Enhancing Your Life through Grateful Living.* Mawmah, NJ: Hidden Springs, an imprint of Paulist Press, 2010.

- www.gratefulness.org. (David Steindl-Rast, PhD, is the founder of the website, which contains a supportive community and many resources for grateful living.)

- https://ggsc.berkeley.edu/. Greater Good Science Center.

ABOUT THE AUTHOR

I n his early college days, Bill Hutcheson dreamed of being a psychiatrist or clinical counselor. By mid-sophomore year, he wrestled with a call to ministry and assumed he would become a Christian counselor. After graduation,  he entered seminary to pursue that passion.

Again, midway through seminary, God caused a 90-degree turn, this time into preparation for the pastorate. Bill graduated with a Master of Divinity in 1980 and moved to South Georgia for his first pastorate. His thirty-eight years of ministry to four congregations were marked by a love of preaching/teaching and an emphasis on helping couples strengthen their marriages.

His initial counseling interests led to the development of an effective and unique process for pre-marriage preparation. Instead of the typical thirty to sixty minutes of preparation from the pastor, Bill worked six to ten hours face-to-face with each couple. The couples also spent a few fun hours doing homework. His emphasis on the marriage, not the wedding, translated to equipping each couple with tools for the marriage road less traveled. Those tools were meant to help the couple build and repair the marriage according to God's plan.

As couples shared their experience with others, Bill received more requests for preparation and occasional marriage enrichment retreats.

In retirement, Bill coaches couples, leads retreats for couple groups, and speaks to congregations who desire happiness in marriage and seek to understand and adopt God's intention for marriage.

His first book, *Marriage Maximized: The Guide to a Purposeful and Passionate Relationship*, captures a process that developed over thirty years. This book picks up after that to help couples grow closer together as spouses and as God's children.

Bill, his bride, Mary Beth, and Myrtle, their "Chiweenie" (a Chihuahua/dachshund mix), live in the beautiful Appalachian foothills of Dahlonega, Georgia. Their two daughters and sons-in-law have given them three terrific grandchildren.

A free ebook edition is available with the purchase of this book.

To claim your free ebook edition:

1. Visit MorganJamesBOGO.com
2. Sign your name CLEARLY in the space
3. Complete the form and submit a photo of the entire copyright page
4. You or your friend can download the ebook to your preferred device

Morgan James BOGO™

A **FREE** ebook edition is available for you or a friend with the purchase of this print book.

_____

CLEARLY SIGN YOUR NAME ABOVE

Instructions to claim your free ebook edition:
1. Visit MorganJamesBOGO.com
2. Sign your name CLEARLY in the space above
3. Complete the form and submit a photo of this entire page
4. You or your friend can download the ebook to your preferred device

Print & Digital Together Forever.

Snap a photo

Free ebook

Read anywhere

Printed in the USA
CPSIA information can be obtained
at www.ICGtesting.com
JSHW021739030224
56563JS00004B/149